Praise for *The 4 Disciplines of Execution for Educators*

4DX is a revolutionary process that has created laser-light focus for staff and students at Hollywood Elementary. Students are learning accountability, responsibility, and practices to successfully meet goals.

—Natalie Macerata, Principal, Hollywood Elementary

As the leader of a diverse district, the 4 Disciplines of Execution has provided a unique and proven formula that continues to assist us in a strategic focus on aligned and sustainable systems prioritizing what is most needed for our stakeholders. From the conception of our District Strategic Plan to individual school goals and lead measures, we have embraced these strategies and principles as the process of our intentional focus that manifests in breakthrough results. This impeccable process will continue to have a lasting impact on our schools, our staff, and our students as they grow and develop personally and academically.

—Dr. Kamela Patton, Superintendent, Collier County Public Schools

The 4DX model has transformed how we teach and learn here at Martin Petitjean Elementary! Our little first-, second-, and third-grade leaders monitor their own learning through this process. Under the direction of our dedicated staff, these leaders set WIGS, and maintain a tracking system within their data portfolios. These young practitioners of this process update classroom, grade-level, and school-wide scoreboards. They know how each one of them fits into the full data system at our school! They are intrinsically motivated through this process and can tell you at any moment exactly how they are performing in all the different data pieces they track. Once you put data into the hands of children, they move the needle. Within this amazing system, we educators are here to facilitate, encourage, and guide. It is truly magical!

—*Kim Cummings, Principal, Martin Petitjean Elementary*

Goals are a very important thing in life and school WIGS can get you really far. When there is something that I need to get done, I try to motivate myself, make a goal out of it and then if I get it done, it'll make me happy. In school I was really struggling with math because I had so many assignments, but my WIGS got me there because I had a goal to complete it. Goals are like motivations and when you complete one it'll make you really happy, I know it will. Trust me.

—*Max Gould, Student, Age 11, Colorado*

In 2018, the Alamo Colleges District became the only higher education, multi-college system, to ever receive the prestigious National Malcolm Baldrige Quality Award. Over the past several years, multiple local, state, and national awards have flowed to the Alamo Colleges, its faculty, staff/administrators, and students, including awards in finance, environment, facility design, academic programs, student success, Early College High Schools, and workforce programs. These awards are a direct result of our implementing The 4 Disciplines of Execution (4DX) starting in 2014 with amazing support from FranklinCovey. Our 450, 4DX teams across our five colleges and district offices resulted in a 244 percent increase in our WIG: student graduation. 4DX drove us to become a dramatically productive, student-focused culture, based on student equity, recruitment, retention, graduation, employment, and baccalaureate achievement. 4DX is the most powerful and effective approach to becoming a high-performing organization because it places the responsibility for high achievement and accountability with the employees, enhances their leadership and understanding of the organization's WIG, and helps employees achieve their goals for student success. My advice to everyone I speak with about our Alamo Colleges' journey to greatness: "Implement 4DX now!"

—*Dr. Bruce Leslie, Chancellor Emeritus, The Alamo Colleges District*

The execution of achievement begins with focus. If the goals aren't clear, then the expectations are not clear, and then you cannot have system-wide accountability for anything because people don't know what they're accountable to. Thanks to the 4 Disciplines, we're clear about what we're working on, everything's aligned to that, and we're getting great results.

—*Candace Singh, Superintendent, Fallbrook Union Elementary School District*

When true implementation of the 4 Disciplines occurs in the classroom, students and teachers can see astounding results because students are focused on their goal and are accountable in ensuring they reach the goal they set. There is nothing more powerful and time-worthy than to teach students how to put into action the 4DX model.

—*Pam Siebenmorgen, Principal, Beard Elementary*

The 4DX model has given my students and me the structure needed to write Wildly Important Goals (WIGs), and accountability in maintaining the tracking of our lead measures and scoreboards. 4DX is not one more thing, but part of our daily classroom routines that have impacted my classroom culture by providing confidence for my students, and has resulted in major growth in my students.

—*Carla Mathis, Classroom Teacher, Beard Elementary*

The accountability piece is a big part of the 4DX model because when you have to report to your peers, it gives you a reason to pursue your goal. Having the visualization of the scoreboard helped keep us on track from week to week. All four components coming together ensured that we met our goals and were successful!

—*Erica Tobin (12th Grade) and Ms. Kate Baskwell (Sports Medicine), Battery Creek High School*

Even at the elementary school level, the 4 Disciplines of Execution provides a foundational foothold and is the basis of our practice. Our team of learners and leaders utilize the methodology within as we structure our strategic plan with an emphasis on educating and nurturing the whole child through actionable steps that yield immediate results. A must-have in every educational environment!

—*Deagon Jewett, Principal, Thornton Creek Elementary*

As students go through the 4DX process, they become so invested in their goals. They see growth and they are motivated to keep going. It ignites a spark in them like I've never seen before, and they are so proud of their accomplishments!

—*Stephanie Kane, Kindergarten Teacher, Lincoln Elementary*

Goals help people make big changes.

—*Sharlette Weliver, Kindergarten Student, Lincoln Elementary*

Also by FranklinCovey

The 4 Disciplines of Execution

The 7 Habits of Highly Effective People

The Leader's Guide to Unconscious Bias

Everyone Deserves a Great Manager

The 5 Choices: The Path to Extraordinary Productivity

Project Management for the Unofficial Project Manager

Also by Sean Covey

The 6 Most Important Decisions You'll Ever Make

The Leader in Me

The 7 Habits of Happy Kids

The 7 Habits of Highly Effective Teens

The 7 Habits of Highly Effective College Students (College Textbook)

The 4 Disciplines of Execution for Educators

ACHIEVING YOUR
WILDLY IMPORTANT GOALS®

SEAN COVEY
New York Times Bestselling Author
LYNN KOSINSKI
MEG THOMPSON

ABOUT FRANKLINCOVEY EDUCATION

For nearly three decades, FranklinCovey Education, a division of FranklinCovey, has been one of the world's most prominent and trusted providers of educational leadership programs and transformational processes. Our mission is to enable greatness in students, teachers, and schools everywhere. The FranklinCovey Education team is primarily composed of outstanding former teachers and administrators from various educational levels and entities.

FranklinCovey is a global, public company specializing in performance improvement. We help organizations and individuals achieve results that require a change in human behavior. Our expertise is in seven areas: Leadership, Execution, Productivity, Trust, Sales Performance, Customer Loyalty, and Education.

For more information about *Leader in Me* or other FranklinCovey Education offerings, please email: educate@franklincovey.com or call: 888-868-1776.

Franklin Covey Co.
2200 W. Parkway Blvd.
Salt Lake City, UT 84119
www.franklincovey.com/education

0418E   EDU2171801 v1.1.1

To educators everywhere, who are committed to making a wildly important difference in the lives of their students.

Table of Contents

SECTION 1: Achieving Your Wildly Important Goals

In this section, we will discuss why goal achievement is so difficult, especially when it involves a lot of people. Also, we will give a short overview of the 4 Disciplines of Execution before we do a deeper dive into each of the 4 Disciplines in section 2.

Introduction

The morning the governor of Florida visited Highlands Elementary School in Immokalee marked a great turning point for the school. Three years before, the school had received an "F" grade from the state for chronic failure to close yawning achievement gaps. Highlands has around 600 students, 98 percent of whom are eligible for free or reduced lunch. Five of six students speak a different language at home, and more than 200 of them come from migrant-worker families. Now, three years after the school adopted the 4 Disciplines, the governor came to Highlands Elementary to congratulate the school for moving from an "F" to an "A."

How did they do it? Laura Mendicino, who was principal at Highlands at the time, credits the 4 Disciplines of Execution. "We always had goals," she said. "Goals were nothing new. But the 'aha' for me was the *combination* of the 4 Disciplines."

"We needed a system of accountability to make sure that we would reach the goals we were setting. We saw the greatness in the 4 Disciplines of Execution—not only the goal setting, but also the tracking, the accountability, the framework for success that was simple to follow for children but also a structure for adults. In the past that was what we were missing. We were very good at setting goals but not so successful at achieving them. We were missing the other pieces: the scoreboarding, the celebrations, the cadence of accountability keeping you going forward."

Welcome to the 4 Disciplines of Execution for Educators

Whether you're a principal, a classroom teacher, a school counselor, a cafeteria worker, a board member, or a bus driver, in a sense you all have the same job—to educate our precious children for rich lives and productive futures. It's the most important job in the world. The only work that compares to it is the work we do in our own homes.

We know you have unique challenges in your job. The challenges of a teacher differ from the superintendent's challenges, and so forth. These challenges differ from class to class, school to school, even nation to nation, but the goal never changes—*to bring about academic improvement and transformation of the whole student that will change the world for the better.*

In contrast to other businesses or organizations, for educators, falling short of achieving that goal can have much more serious and lasting consequences. If we fall short as a society, the loss of potential and the impoverishing of the lives of our students can be truly heartbreaking. By contrast, achieving that goal can be the most joyous, most fruitful, most satisfying of triumphs. Truly, much is at stake.

Everyone agrees on the goal; unfortunately, attaining that goal can be "hit and miss" in the whirlwind of the world we live in.

How can we reach that goal? How can we avoid falling short?

These questions are always foremost in mind for educators. Here is the challenge:

It's one thing to set a goal.
It's another thing to achieve it.

This challenge is universal. How many politicians set lofty goals for public schools that are never attained? How many Strategic Improvement Plans gather dust on a shelf somewhere or get buried in a digital dumping ground? How many teachers start the school year with great expectations but barely hang on in a whirlwind of demands, disasters, and disappointments?

As an educator, many of your challenges are beyond your control. However, there are two things you can influence: the goals you set and the execution of the goals. Which do you think people struggle with the most?

You're right. It's the execution of the goals.

In comparison to execution, goal setting is easy. Most people know how to set goals. They do it all the time. For example, most educators know all about SMART goals, where SMART means "Specific, Measurable, Attainable, Relevant, and Time-Bound." Everybody sets SMART goals for reaching proficiency levels, winning a championship, reducing a drop-out rate, and so forth.

But few people know how to execute them. That's the hard part.

That's what this book is about. Here you will learn the 4 Disciplines of Execution, a process that has been embraced by thousands of primary and secondary schools, colleges, and universities around the globe as a methodology for setting and reaching their goals. Here you'll discover that it takes more than being SMART to achieve a goal. As Highlands Elementary in Florida discovered while progressing from an "F" to an "A" grade, it takes discipline: in fact, it takes the 4 Disciplines.

How many times have you set a goal for your district, school, or classroom only to find that it was soon smothered by competing priorities or just the sheer demand of keeping your head above water? How many times have you said to yourself, "Someday, things are going to change around here," only to find they don't?

We believe all that can change. Here's our promise to you. If done with fidelity, the 4 Disciplines will help you achieve your most important goals, perhaps for the first time. In addition to achieving your goals, you will overcome hurdles and obstacles that you've never been able to conquer before. You will dramatically increase the engagement levels of all stakeholders in your school, and you will grow in confidence that your hard work can actually produce predictable and sustainable results. As you do this, you will gain the satisfaction of achieving something that is measurably, demonstrably, and "wildly" important.

The 4 Disciplines Of Execution: An Overview

I remember it like it was yesterday. I was a recently transferred, fairly new teacher attending a faculty meeting three months into the school year. The topic of the meeting was something called "school improvement goals." School improvement goals were the last thing on my mind. I was still trying to figure out the new reading curriculum. I tried to focus, pretended to be interested, and then I asked a question that silenced the room: "What goals are you talking about? And what should I be doing about them?" I had a feeling we were all quietly asking ourselves the same things.

The principal tilted her head down and glared right through me over the top of her glasses. In a voice that would make a bulldog cower, she proceeded to ask me how I could possibly not know the school improvement goals and strategies. After all, they had been handed out during the opening faculty meeting with strict instructions to implement them.

Oh, *that* was it. I had gotten all those handouts in that meeting they held the day before students arrived—the same day they handed me my revised class list for the third time. Sometime in between making and tearing up name tags, pleading with the custodian for more desks, and preparing for an engaging, team-building opening day of school, I was supposed to absorb the School Improvement Plan with its many goals and strategies. The plan that, by the way, nobody ever talked about again until that unforgettable "staff meeting of shame" months later. We didn't hear much about it even after that.

Over the course of many years in education, my role in PreK-12 education changed several times. However, I would see this pattern of failed School Improvement Plans repeated time and time again.

By way of this book, our goal is to help you break that pattern so you and your colleagues can set meaningful goals and achieve them together. We hope to help you gain insights about where your plan might be falling short and how to get back on track toward reaching your goals.

Let's get started with a story.

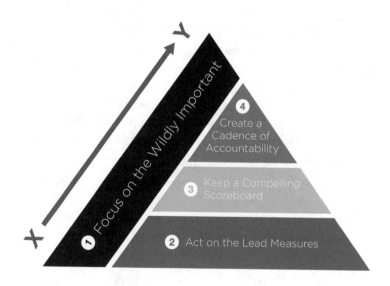

The 4 Disciplines of Execution is a system for getting the most important things done. As illustrated, Discipline 1 is about identifying the most important goal we have to achieve, and it is supported by Disciplines 2, 3, and 4.

Lekha teaches English to 215 students in a suburban middle school in the United States. For her, writing is such an important skill that she assigns her students to write a short essay nearly every week. Over the 36 weeks of the school year, Lekha analyzes, corrects, and grades around 7,000 pieces of student writing. If she invests a mere 15 minutes into each paper, she will devote the equivalent of 218 workdays each school year to evaluating her students' work. She will do this on top of 182 days teaching her classes. So, Lekha's workload adds up to 400 days per year out of 365.

Obviously, Lekha can't devote 15 minutes per week to providing written feedback to each of her students. There's not enough time in the year. Ten minutes would add up to 145 extra workdays. Better, but still every day would be a 14-hour day for Lekha. So, she settles for 5 minutes per paper, which adds only 72 extra workdays per year. She knows very well that 5 minutes isn't nearly enough to give meaningful coaching to a student.

Furthermore, Lekha lives in a whirlwind of administrative chores, extra-curricular assignments (she coaches volleyball), and parent conferences. Her job is crushing. She went into teaching excited about her subject, yearning to make a difference, but she's feeling battered. She's getting tired, sleepless, and easily irritated. Some say she's "burning out."

"Most jobs in the 'real world' have a gap between what would be nice and what is possible. The tragedy for teachers is that the gap is a chasm, not crossed by reasonable and judicious adjustments," according to educational authority Ted Sizer. If educators complain about their workload, "they find no seriously empathetic audience." Most of them "just let it all continue, a conspiracy, a toleration of a chasm between the necessary and the provided and acceptance of big rhetoric and little reality."[1]

Educators like Lekha rarely "burn out"; that would suggest they have nothing left to give. But they are often demoralized because they cannot do the job the way they believe is right. "The better and more accurate story is that teachers want to engage in good work that benefits students, communities, and the profession, and they become frustrated when they cannot do so," says education professor Doris Santoro.[2]

We often talk about "closing a gap" in educational performance. But often the gap between doing the job right and settling for mediocre results is a *chasm*.

What is the job to be done?

How do we cross the chasm between achieving superb results and just getting by?

Every school system has a job to be done. For some, the job is defined by government entities that require a certain level of student proficiency by a certain time. A school succeeds if it achieves those levels. Others must overcome serious challenges, such as poverty or absenteeism. Often, a successful school is driven by a compelling mission or vision.

Because schools are such complicated places, jumping the chasm can feel like an overpowering challenge. It's such a big jump that Lekha and millions of educators like her lose sight of the peak of greatness they aspire to. One of our colleagues shares this story with us:

I was chair of the community council for my local high school, and we as a council developed a serious goal of improving test scores. My job was to orient the teachers to the new goal, so I made an appointment with the faculty to explain what we were doing and get things started.

At first I was baffled—the teachers didn't seem to be listening to me. Slowly, I figured out why. On one teacher's desk was a stack that looked like a thousand papers. It was just one day's collection of essays he would have to evaluate and grade. Plus, he had a parent conference to go to and the next day's lessons to plan. He looked kind of helpless as I jabbered on and on, but he wasn't really listening. There wasn't room in his brain for this, and I didn't blame him!

If you are an educational leader who wants to reach a significant goal, you will eventually have to face this reality. Will staff members be fully engaged in your goal? No. It's not because they don't want to be. They are just trying to do their best within the system. Like Lekha, they are already on task all the time.

Your life as an educational professional is a whirlwind of competing priorities. Countless urgencies press on your time. Some are critical emergencies, such as a security threat or a student in crisis. Some people demand your attention *right now*. Preparing, evaluating, conferencing, counseling—there is no end to the urgencies. It's like being in the middle of a tornado with stuff flying past your eyes at top speed.

It's so hard to make significant progress under these conditions.

But it can be done. Thousands of schools worldwide are doing it now—achieving goals they never thought possible, shattering barriers to success they thought were indestructible, and gaining the confidence that they can succeed again and again no matter the circumstances.

The key is a set of disciplines based on timeless, unchanging principles that always work: The 4 Disciplines of Execution.

1. Focus on the Wildly Important

2. Act on Lead Measures

3. Keep a Compelling Scoreboard

4. Create a Cadence of Accountability

We intuitively work against these 4 Disciplines. Because they may not feel natural to us, we are sometimes inclined to do the opposite. Typically, we lack focus, we don't track our progress, and we don't hold ourselves accountable for progress. It's hard enough just to do our day job.

Although the 4 Disciplines are counterintuitive, they work. The 4 Disciplines of Execution (4DX) is a system that has been proven across decades of experience with thousands of organizations. We've learned through experience that professional people want to win. They want to make a contribution that matters, and 4DX enables them to do that. The 4DX system works because it is based on principles, not practices. Practices are situational, subjective, and always evolving. But principles are timeless and self-evident, and they apply everywhere to everyone all the time. They are laws that are just as natural as gravity. Whether you understand them or even agree with them doesn't matter—they still apply.

The timeless principles of execution have always been focus, leverage, engagement, and accountability. They are inescapable principles of effectiveness. As you overview the 4 Disciplines below, you will see how these principles work in practice.

Discipline 1: Focus on the Wildly Important

Some goals are important, but only a few are "Wildly Important Goals." We call them WIGs. These are the goals that must be achieved or nothing else really matters very much by comparison. A WIG is different than a PIG. PIG's are Pretty Important Goals, and every organization has lots of them. But every organization also has a goal that is wildly important and no other success can compensate for failing to achieve it. It may be a goal around attendance, student behavior, literacy and math proficiency, or degrees earned. It is the goal that is staring us in the face and just has to get done.

Discipline 1 is based on the principle of focus. If you focus the sun's rays on a piece of paper, it will burn. The same is true of people—once focused on a collective challenge, their passions are ignited and there's little they can't accomplish.

For example, Blossom School in Indonesia was failing because some people didn't consider it important to be "on time." Chronic tardiness too often cut into instructional time. Teachers had to stop to re-teach students who arrived late and wasted about half the available instructional time. The problem was simple—if students weren't there, they couldn't learn. But solving the problem was *not* simple.

The school chose punctuality as a Wildly Important Goal: students would be there at the beginning of class at least 70 percent of the time. The school began to require on-time attendance in order to join a lesson. If students were late, they were expected to wait for their next class and catch up on the lesson on their own time. Although students and parents resisted this change, Blossom School persisted. Within three years, they surpassed a 70-percent on-time goal and ultimately reached 98 percent.

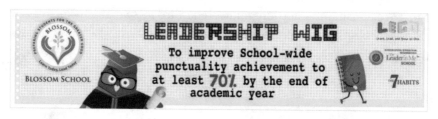

A lack of punctuality was cutting seriously into instructional time at this school. So they set a Wildly Important Goal to make measurable improvement and found that most other important measures also improved.

Intense focus on a Wildly Important Goal made all the difference. The students were in class on time and all the time instead of only half the time. This success allowed the school to move forward on many other initiatives that were important to it.

Once you identify the WIG, the next question is how to achieve the WIG.

Discipline 2: Act on Lead Measures

Educators deal with lag measures all the time: grades, test scores, attendance, behavior, graduation rates. Once you see these lag measures, there's nothing you can do about them—they're history. To achieve a goal, you must act on the *lead* measures—those actions you can take that will predict and influence success of a goal.

Discipline 2 is based on the principle of leverage—that some actions are more impactful than others. A lead measure is simply an action that is most likely to get the results you want. The question is, what can you do daily or weekly that will influence the achievement of the WIG?

You can aim for a 90 percent graduation rate, but you can't control it. So, what can you control? Your own actions. In Discipline 2, you choose actions that will have the most impact on reaching the goal, and you track those actions. Those are your lead measures.

For example, the faculty at Seven Hills Elementary School in Texas knew their students weren't meeting the district WIG of 90 percent reading proficiency. So, they had to discover a lead measure that would have the most impact on the goal. They decided the staff needed more professional development in literacy, so they set aside time and resources to get trained. The additional learning made the difference. As they grew more confident and more capable, the staff met the goal and exceeded it.

Once you identify the lag measure for the WIG and the lead measures that will bring it about, you track both measures consistently on a scoreboard, which is the next discipline.

Discipline 3: Keep a Compelling Scoreboard

A game becomes real when you start keeping score. When you don't keep score, nobody knows or cares how things are going. What if bowlers couldn't see the pins or football players couldn't see the score? They would get disengaged really fast. The reality is people play much differently when they're keeping score.

A compelling scoreboard is visible. Everyone can see it at all times. It shows the lead and lag measures. It shows where you started, where you are in closing the gap, and where you will end. Within only a few seconds, a compelling scoreboard tells you whether you are winning or losing. The scoreboard helps you to know if your lead measure is working. Most of all, it motivates everyone to make progress and helps you decide whether to speed up, slow down, or continue as you are.

Discipline 3 is based on the principle of engagement. When people know if they are winning or losing, they get more engaged in their work. A compelling scoreboard isn't only for the coaches, it is also for the players. It is public and visible for all to see.

A scoreboard like the one below is fun and shows the students and staff where they are in relation to the goal. When the goal line gets to the top of the animals' heads, the goal has been reached and there will be a big celebration. Celebrating success is an important part of the 4 Disciplines.

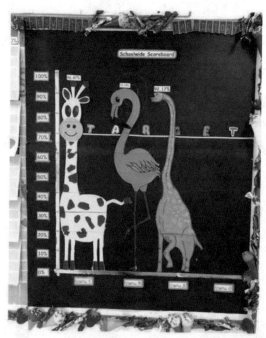

This scoreboard is compelling because it shows where the students are in their quest to reach their goal and how much further they need to go.

Discipline 4: Create a Cadence of Accountability

Unfortunately, everybody has made a goal in life, only to forget about it (which explains all the jokes about New Year's resolutions and failed diets). Goals do not achieve themselves; the people who are accountable for the goal should meet *regularly* and *frequently* to account for their progress. Because this meeting is regular, we call it a "cadence of accountability." A "cadence" is how often a regularly scheduled thing happens. A weekly or even daily cadence is essential if you're going to stay focused on the goal.

Discipline 4 is based on the principle of accountability. Unless we hold each other strictly accountable for the goal all of the time, our goals and efforts will get sucked into the whirlwind of our day-to-day urgencies and priorities.

The students update the animal board shown every day and talk about what they will do to move further toward the goal line. It becomes an exciting game for them.

If you keep the cadence going, you are more likely to achieve the WIG.

When practiced intentionally and effectively, these four simple disciplines can make all the difference to your success. The power is in the system. Take away any of the disciplines and the system collapses. They seem quite obvious on the surface, but as we go deeper into each one, you'll see that they are common sense but not common practice. And you'll discover, as so many educators have, that they work. It doesn't matter if you're talking about a classroom full of students, a department, a school faculty, or an entire district. When people:

1. Know what the "Wildly Important Goal" is,

2. Know what to do to achieve the goal,

3. Know the score at all times, and

4. Hold themselves accountable regularly and frequently for the results,

—something remarkable happens. They cross the chasm Ted Sizer talks about. They make a habit of reaching "Wildly Important Goals." Lekha gets focused on what matters most and backs out of the whirlwind of demands and frustrations that are consuming her energies. She achieves what she set out to achieve as an educator.

Besides feeling satisfied at achieving something important, educators who practice the 4 Disciplines feel liberated. Having a methodology for executing on your goals makes your life so much easier. Students take more ownership of their learning. Teachers get clear on the real priorities. Administrators free themselves from minutiae and focus on helping students. "We've complicated teachers' lives for long enough," says education scholar Mike Schmoker. "It is time to simplify their work in ways that make them *more* effective, but with less effort and frustration."[3]

In addition to helping classrooms, schools, and districts achieve their goals, the 4 Disciplines teach students a methodology for goal setting and goal achievement that they can use in every area of their lives for the rest of their lives. Educators who practice the Disciplines discover that their students are not only closing achievement gaps but also learning a systematic way to shape their own future intentionally instead of haphazardly. In this respect, the 4 Disciplines produce a significant Paradigm Shift, or change of mindset, in everyone who implements them from educator to student. Laura Mendicino observes, "The first year we put it in place and saw the closing of the achievement gaps—and the students' ability to articulate what they were doing to reach the goal, what they were doing to succeed in their lives—my whole mindset shifted. I was excited to see a system that would enable them to be successful not only academically but in life."

Educators want to succeed. They want to make a meaningful difference. They don't go into education for the money, but to make a difference in the lives of these young students. If they can't do the job they want to do, they become demoralized. But if they are freed to focus on and achieve what really matters, they engage, re-energize, and thrive.

SECTION 2:
The 4 Disciplines of Execution

In this section, we will take a deeper dive into each of the four disciplines.

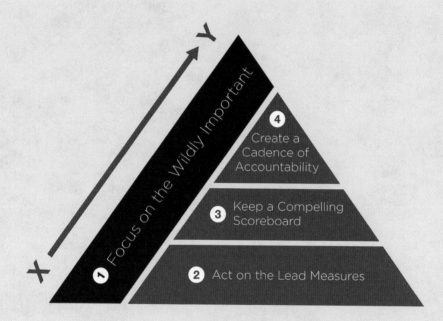

DISCIPLINE 1:
Focus on the Wildly Important

The enemy of the best is the good.

Karl, the principal of a large elementary school, sat back and looked over his laptop screen with satisfaction. It was 7 o'clock in the morning, and he had already finished entering his "goals" into the "SIP"—the Strategic Improvement Plan. He was ahead of schedule! The plan wasn't due at the district office until 8 o'clock.

He admired his goals. He had carefully crafted dozens of them. Not even Ms. Rigorista, a sixth-grade teacher down the hall who was always correcting his grammar, could fault them. They were well written, culturally sensitive, and loaded with the right jargon. He especially liked these:

- Foster a cycle of continuous instructional improvement through the use of data, collaboration, and instructional support.
- Narrow achievement gaps with respect to race, ethnicity, and socioeconomic status and increase the achievement of students with special needs.
- Ensure all students become knowledgeable, responsible, caring, and contributing members of society.
- Engage parents and the school community through face-to-face communication and digital means.
- Promote and support effective use of technology for curriculum and instruction, and ensure reliable and efficient technology infrastructure.
- Improve our mathematics summative scores.

Karl had never felt so ready for next week's faculty meeting when he would unveil these goals to the staff. For once, he was on top of the SIP. As usual, he had dreaded the task, but this time he felt pretty good about it. And once it was in the hands of the superintendent, he wouldn't have to worry about it for another two years.

Just then the custodian came into his office. "We'll have to call a plumber. The toilets in the boys' restroom are overflowing. Somebody tried to flush paper towels down them."

So, another day began for Karl. After checking on the plumbing, he had to call an irate parent who was complaining about a teacher. Then he patrolled the halls to get wandering students into class, made announcements, caught two students fighting, monitored the cafeteria, watched football practice, tried to stay awake through the evening choir concert, and was home by 9 p.m., exhausted.

The Whirlwind

What are the odds that Karl will achieve his Strategic Improvement goals if his days are all like this? What are the odds he will remember his dozen Strategic Improvement goals a week from now? Or even tomorrow?

To ask these questions is not to fault Karl. An educator's life is a whirlwind of days like his. Superintendents, teachers, principals, counselors, coaches—they deal with constantly shifting demands every day. The multiplicity of tasks could make anyone's head spin.

So, how do you achieve Strategic Improvement goals in the middle of such a whirlwind?

Nearly every district school has some sort of Strategic Improvement Plan. Often the authorities require it. Many governmental entities mandate extensive and often detailed plans for public schools. Private schools usually have similar plans. Plans typically call for improved academics, teacher development, and community involvement.

Outside of formal district and school plans, individual teachers, departments, and professional learning communities usually set goals for themselves. Most educators are idealistic people eager to do good things for their students, so they are natural goal setters.

However, educational goals often go unmet. Strategic Improvement Plans frequently fail. Pundits point with alarm at stagnating test scores.

Huge grants are received by districts but years later have little to show for them. Presidents propose ambitious educational reforms that have little impact. Reformers claim that their policies will boost educational performance, while their plans "deliver few benefits and often harm the very students they purport to help."[4]

The problem is not with the optimism and zeal of the educational community. Rather, the problem is with the *whirlwind* of demands on our time and our lives.

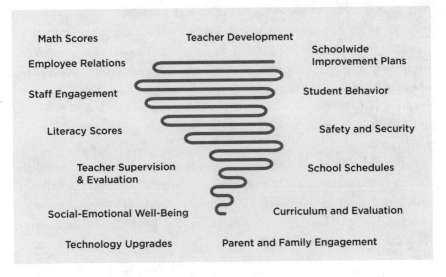

Math Scores   Teacher Development   Schoolwide Improvement Plans

Employee Relations   Student Behavior

Staff Engagement

Literacy Scores   Safety and Security

Teacher Supervision & Evaluation   School Schedules

Social-Emotional Well-Being   Curriculum and Evaluation

Technology Upgrades   Parent and Family Engagement

Educators live in a whirlwind of demands on their time. It's difficult to focus on any one goal in the midst of so many priorities.

We are simply *trying to do too much*. Listen to education scholar Isobel Stevenson, who helps schools write improvement plans.

"Most of us are unrealistic about what it will take to get things done, so we list more priorities than we can possibly accomplish in the given time frame. One of the exercises I use with leadership teams is to ask them to write every initiative going on in their districts on a different sticky note. Often, they cover an entire piece of chart paper with sticky notes, which is a pretty good indication that they're trying to do too many things at once."[5]

We find the same thing in our work with educational leaders all over the world. They have too many competing priorities pulling everyone in disparate directions. As the whirlwind of job responsibilities continues to grow, the inability to focus impedes results.

Because of the pressure to account for concrete results, schools are now flooded with accountability measures—federal, state, district assessments, standards, "school grades," online ratings and reviews—and more. You almost need a math degree to handle all the numbers required in a Strategic Improvement Plan. As the following observers note, these numbers can make school improvement harder instead of easier:

"Too often, data—far from empowering schools—leave schools and teachers feeling overwhelmed, realizing that they need to make drastic improvements but unsure where to begin. As a result, schools often try to make too many improvements at once, drafting comprehensive improvement plans that change instructional programs, alter scheduling, and revamp organizational and support structures. Such plans throw everything but the kitchen sink at the problem; in trying to do everything at once, they often do nothing well and bring little or no gains in student achievement."[6]

The whirlwind of expanding responsibilities combined with the flood of data make "school improvement" seem a formidable challenge. Still, the increasing availability of data can work to your advantage if you look at it through the lens of Discipline 1. Once you define your most important goals, you can now measure progress in ways you never could before.

So, the key to achieving something wildly important is to pluck it out of the whirlwind of the day job and give it disproportionate focus. The day job will always be there and will take most of your time, but if you give increased focus to that WIG you can accomplish what may seem impossible.

Wildly Important Goals

As we have said, some goals are more important than others. And a few goals are "wildly" important. We define a "Wildly Important Goal" (a WIG) as a goal that you must reach or nothing else you achieve really matters very much. For example, if students are not learning to read, it doesn't much matter if they are wearing the prescribed school uniform: The school is failing at its primary purpose.

Practicing Discipline 1: Focus on the Wildly Important means narrowing your focus to one or two (preferably one and never more than three) highly important goals so you can manageably achieve them in the midst of the whirlwind of the day job. Simply put, Discipline 1 is about applying more energy against fewer goals because, when it comes to setting goals, the law of diminishing returns is as real as the law of gravity.

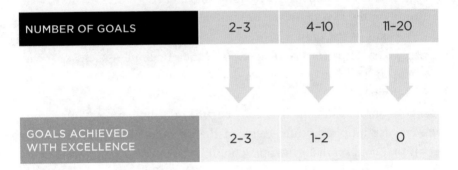

NUMBER OF GOALS	2–3	4–10	11–20
GOALS ACHIEVED WITH EXCELLENCE	2–3	1–2	0

If a school focuses on two or even three goals beyond the demands of their whirlwind, they can often accomplish these goals with excellence. However, if they set four to ten goals, our experience has been that they will achieve only one or two. They'll be going backward! If they go after 11-20 in addition to the whirlwind, they'll lose focus. And our experience is that most schools and organizations usually have more than 10 goals or top priorities they are trying to get done. Our friend Karl had a dozen lofty goals to pursue! With all those goals added to the mix, the whirlwind just gets bigger and stronger. Confronted with so many goals, everyone will stop listening—let alone executing.

Why is this so?

The fundamental principle behind Discipline 1 is the principle of focus, the natural law that we've all experienced that tells us that to be effective at something we must concentrate energy on that thing. The opposite of focus is to have our attention be all over the place, be spread out, or diffused. The reality is that human beings are genetically hardwired to do one thing at a time with excellence.

You're probably thinking–proudly–that you're great at multitasking and can get a lot of things done at the same time. However, science tells us the human brain can give full focus to only a single object at any given moment. You can't put your best effort into driving a car while talking on your phone and eating a burger. The same is true about juggling multiple important school goals at once. Our elementary school principal Karl will never be able to achieve any of the goals he has set if he tries to achieve them all at once.

MIT neuroscientist Earl Miller says the brain can't even focus on as few as two tasks at once. "The real problem occurs when we try to concentrate on the two tasks we are dealing with, because this then causes an overload of the brain's processing capacity. This is particularly true when we try to perform similar tasks at the same time—such as writing an email and talking on the phone—as they compete to use the same part of the brain. As a result, your brain simply slows down."[7]

If the brain can't simultaneously focus on simple tasks like processing emails and phone calls, think of the impact of losing focus on the goals that could transform your school!

The prefrontal cortex of the brain is designed to deal with smaller bits of information rather than the barrage of information we constantly throw at it. In a Stanford University experiment, researchers tested 49 people who do a lot of media multitasking and 52 who don't. "The heavy multitaskers performed poorly on all the tests. They were more easily distracted, had less control over their attention, and were much less able to distinguish important information from trivia." Professor Clifford Nass, who conducted the study, concluded, "Everything distracts them."[8]

The primary task is the WIG. The more intense your whirlwind, the more you need to focus to achieve the WIG. The busier you are, the more critical it is to move from the conventional thinking to 4DX thinking of focusing on the "wildly important."

CONVENTIONAL THINKING	4DX THINKING
All of our goals are Priority 1. We can successfully multitask and succeed at five, ten, or fifteen important goals or initiatives. All we need to do is work smarter not harder.	Many of our goals are important, but only one or two are wildly important. We call them WIGs. They are the goals we must achieve. Our finest effort can only be given to one or two Wildly Important Goals at a time.

Suppose you're a passenger on an airplane about to land. Do you want the air-traffic controller to be focusing on your plane or on all of the other planes in the sky? The controller's job is to land one plane at a time while other planes are circling. You wouldn't want it any other way—especially if you're on that one plane. When you focus on the wildly important, everything else that is important—your day job—will take care of itself over time. These other important things are like planes circling and waiting in the air. But the air traffic controller can only land one plane at a time. The same is true for goals.

Why is there so much pressure to set many goals when it makes better sense to focus on a few?

Educators answer to multiple stakeholders—government officials, district leaders, parents, board members, owners, and, most important, students. Each stakeholder group, while sharing a common interest in student development, often has different agendas and measures of success. School leaders are pressed to satisfy all these stakeholders. They're expected to find solutions to the social, emotional, and academic needs of their students. In addition, modern schooling is incredibly complex, with many variables that can impact success. Under this immense pressure, it is no wonder educators have difficulty prioritizing one goal over another.

Government accountability requirements further reinforce the expectation that school leaders must fix voids in the school culture, address social-emotional readiness, increase proficiency rates, and close the performance gaps for subgroups. That's why Strategic Improvement Plans often exceed 30 pages.

Now you might be asking, "With so many demands on me, how can I possibly narrow my focus to one or two WIGs?"

We believe all leaders should display this quotation in a prominent place: "There will always be more good ideas than there is capacity to execute."

We understand you are asked, even required, to set numerous goals. However, we can't overemphasize the importance of focusing on only one or two *Wildly* Important Goals at once. As Stephen R. Covey said, "You have to decide what your highest priorities are and have the courage–pleasantly, smilingly, unapologetically–to say no to other things.

And the way you do that is by having a bigger 'yes' burning inside."

Saying "yes to the important" doesn't mean you are throwing away everything else. If you decide that improving literacy scores is the single most important thing you have to do, it doesn't mean that you don't care about the culture of the school, or parent involvement, or teacher development. Those issues are still out there, and you will give them the attention they need and deserve as part of your whirlwind or your day job. "Improving literary scores" is like the plane you are landing right now, but it doesn't mean you aren't paying attention to the other planes circling in the sky, so to speak. It's just that you are going to be giving some extra, ultra-focused time and attention to that one thing that will make all the difference and has to get done!

Once you find your 'yes'—your focus—you can decide where to invest your finest energies.

So, what is "wildly important" for you? What is your "burning yes"? How do you decide which of many possible goals should be your WIG?

Often, the choice of a WIG is obvious. If your district's existence is threatened by financial or environmental or performance issues, survival is the WIG. At other times, competing priorities or even politics can enter into the choice. For example, one teacher might say, "I'm telling you, reading proficiency is the most important thing, and it should be our WIG!" Another chimes in, "Don't forget, without math mastery, our students have no future." "I'm sorry, but you're way off," says a third. "Security is the most important thing. In this day and age, our schools are in constant danger."

The problem here is that the team is asking the wrong question. Don't ask, "What's the most important thing we should be doing?"

Instead, begin by asking "If everything else stayed the same, what change would have the most impact on accomplishing our mission as a district or school?" This question should clear up some of the confusion.

Your WIG might come from outside the whirlwind. Consider what you're trying to accomplish. Ask yourself the big strategic questions: What's your vision or mission? What do you want to be? How do you see the school in five years? Contemplate the "big picture" that you rarely get to think about because you're being blown around by the whirlwind.

Your WIG might also come from inside the whirlwind. What wastes too much of your time that you could be investing in more important priorities? What's broken that must be fixed? Are you being eaten alive by issues with physical facilities? Is there deep distrust between faculty and administration? Do you have a behavior or an attendance problem?

Martin Petitjean School in Louisiana was floundering because of a lack of attendance. At this Title 1 school, a large percentage of the students simply didn't show up for school. Everything suffered because of this—academics, behavior, community and staff relationships. After learning about the 4 Disciplines, Dr. Kimberly Cummins, the principal, knew that her wildly important priority had to be fixing the attendance problem.

Dr. Cummins and her staff focused hard on attendance, setting a WIG of 97 percent daily attendance. This school WIG percolated down until every classroom had its own attendance WIG. By practicing the 4 Disciplines, they eventually achieved and managed to maintain an average of 96–97 percent attendance each year. Being on time at school became wildly important in the minds of students and teachers alike.

One morning, a man brought first-grade student named Mario to school tardy. As the man was about to fill out the sign-in book, he asked the office staff the name of the student. According to Dr. Cummins:

We looked at him in shock. "You don't know who you brought to school?" we asked. He said, "No—the little guy was running along the road and asked me for a ride to school. I agreed to bring him. I don't know him, but I felt bad because he really wanted to come to school." We thanked the man for bringing him, and then we had a talk with Mario.

It turned out that Mario had missed the bus. When he awoke and realized he was late, he tried to wake his mother to take him to school. She refused to get up and told him to just stay home. He put on his uniform, grabbed his backpack, and went outside. He ran up the street looking for someone to drive him to school. This gentleman was passing in his car and agreed to take him. Mario didn't know the man, but he had seen him in the neighborhood before. Mario told us, "I have to be here! Our class has to have perfect attendance—it is one of our goals. If I'm not here, I mess it up for the whole class!"

We hugged Mario and thanked him for caring so much about his class attendance WIG that he went to that much trouble. We, of course, also emphasized to him that he should never again ask a stranger for a ride.

This kind of devotion to the attendance WIG helped Martin Petit-jean School to win the National Blue Ribbon Award for closing their significant achievement gap. More significantly, every program at the school benefits because the students are *there* consistently.

In another instance, the staff at the rural Alcester-Hudson Elementary School in rural South Dakota were "surprised, embarrassed, and humiliated" when the state downgraded them to a "school that needs improvement." Only 55 percent of students tested as proficient in reading and 45 percent in math. Devastated at the many data points that showed they were "underperforming," they didn't know which problem to tackle first. To make things worse, they had lost their principal to budget cuts.

So, the Alcester-Hudson teachers took control of the school. Although they were not aware of the 4 Disciplines, they practiced the principles behind them without knowing it. Wisely, they used the data to focus on one problem at a time. Reasoning that the most impactful issue was reading, the teachers set a reading-proficiency target for each student at each grade level. "After a year of consistently focusing on instructional goals and discussing each student's achievement, the teachers were gratified to see scores on the state standardized tests rise significantly."

With this "quick win" behind them, they went back to the data to decide what the next focus should be. "Teachers grew so adept at using data that they were able to use formative assessments to monitor each student's learning in relation to state and district content standards." Within three years, 94 percent of students achieved "proficiency" in math and 100 percent in reading on state assessments.[9] That's how intense focus can pay off.

Regardless of the form your Strategic Improvement Plan takes, you can focus your energies on the wildly important. You might have to fill in box after box on a many-faceted SIP

Strategic Improvement Plan

1–2
Wildly Important Goals
(WIGs)

Effective schools filter the strategic plan down to one or two WIGs.

template, but *your* priorities are *yours*. Put your WIGs into the SIP, but don't feel constrained by the SIP. As Bruce Leslie, a 4DX disciple and former president of the Alamo Colleges District in Texas, says, "We're all used to 300-page strategic plans in a book that nobody reads. But we had our strategic plan on one page. We had all the important measures in one place."

If a college system with 100,000 students can reduce their plan to one page, surely an elementary or a high school can do the same.

Identify Your WIGs

A Wildly Important Goal is a goal that can make all the difference.

All school systems, districts, and individual schools have goals, often too many. So, how do you choose what's wildly important? Your Strategic Improvement Plan will suggest certain WIGs. As we've said, sometimes the choice of a WIG is obvious. Other times, you will choose a goal that—everything else being equal—will make the most impact on improving your school.

Use this tool to select a Wildly Important Goal:

1. Brainstorm together with your colleagues a list of candidate WIGs. Don't assume beforehand what they should be. Do not reject, criticize, or choose ideas prematurely. Listen carefully to each proposal. Start each idea with a verb. Why? Because a goal is an *action* you will take.

2. Rank the candidate WIGs in order of impact. Ask people to vote and explain their votes. Listen carefully to their reasoning.

3. Select a few candidate WIGs based on the group input and your personal judgment.

4. Experiment on these candidate WIGs. Ask other people for input. Research what other schools have done about the issues. Analyze the data available to you to gain a greater understanding of the issues.

BRAINSTORM WIGS	RANK	SELECT CANDIDATES	SELECT WIGS
Verb...			
Verb...			
Verb...			
Verb...			
Verb...			
Verb...			

Data analysis might lead to reframing the WIG. While analyzing reading data, for example, you might find that one subgroup of students lags the rest of the school, so moving them forward becomes your WIG.

Digging still deeper, you might find their attendance is low, so getting them to class becomes the WIG.

5. Choose your WIG(s). After fully mining your data and carefully reflecting on the real job to be done as a school, don't ask "What's most important?" Ask instead, "If we could choose only one of these candidate WIGs, which would have the most impact?" This question changes the way you think and lets you clearly identify the focus that would make all the difference.

Here's an example of what Karl might have done with his candidate WIGs by using this tool. He and his staff could list ideas, prioritize them on a scale from 1 (most important) to 10, then select the most impactful ideas to experiment with.

BRAINSTORM WIGS	RANK	SELECT CANDIDATES	SELECT WIGS
Use data to drive continuous improvement.	3	Narrow achievement gaps.	Focus on narrowing achievement gaps by using a data-driven continuous-improvement model.
Narrow achievement gaps across racial and economic lines.	1		
Do character education to improve student citizenship values.	2	Do character education.	
Set up communication networks with parents and non-parent groups.	4		
Update our instructional technology with better streaming capabilities.	5	Do data-driven continuous improvement.	
Construct new media center to include tech as well as books.	6		

In the end, Karl's school combined two candidate WIGs into one.

Rules for Focusing on the Wildly Important

Narrowing the focus of a group of students, not to mention an entire educational community, is a big task. It becomes easier if you follow these rules for focusing on the "wildly important."

- Focus on no more than one to three WIGs at a time—preferably one.
- Align your WIGs to the WIGs of your leaders.
- Collaborate on choosing WIGs.
- Define "From X to Y by When."

Focus on no more than one to three WIGs at a time—preferably one. Remember the phrase, "Jack of all trades, master of none." You don't want to be Jack. The key to Discipline 1 is not to overload any single leader, team, or individual performer. The goal is to be so keenly focused, that instead of addressing many goals but achieving none, you focus on one or two goals that can be successfully met. If you violate this rule, you will have lost your focus as a team. Of course, you have other concerns to work on, but you invest in your WIG the finest energy and resources you have.

Recall this inescapable fact: *Human beings are genetically hardwired to do only one thing at a time with excellence.* Therefore, your finest effort should be reserved for the one thing that matters most.

Align your WIGs to the WIGs of your leaders. Most schools belong to districts or larger organizations that set goals or direct or guide the selection of site-based WIGs. All WIGs should align to the WIGs of a higher authority. It won't work if the school has a reading WIG and the third-grade teachers have a math WIG. The purpose of WIGs at lower levels in the organization is to help achieve WIGs at higher levels.

For example, at the board and district levels, Michigan's Northville Public Schools set a WIG that all students would meet a certain standard of reading proficiency within a set period of time. At the school level, Winchester Elementary chose to focus specifically on non-fiction text. At one grade level, the WIG was that students would identify the main idea and supporting details of a non-fiction text at least 83 percent of the time. Finally, individual students had their own reading-proficiency WIGs. This thoughtfully aligned and cascaded planning ensures everyone is working toward a common end. If WIGs are aligned at all levels—student level, class level, grade level, school level, and district level—it's amazing what can be accomplished.

The Alamo Colleges District in Texas, which we mentioned earlier, is one of the largest community-college systems in the United States, with five campuses serving about 100,000 students in the greater San Antonio area. There are some 5,300 faculty and staff in 450 departments. Former President Bruce Leslie says, "We often get criticized for trying to do too many things, and that's true of many schools. But with the 4 Disciplines in place, we had 450 teams with 450 different WIGs, all aligned to one overarching WIG: increasing our graduation rate. It was amazing."

How can everyone in such a large and complex institution as Alamo get to this level of goal alignment? It took about two years. At first, leaders focused on getting the academic departments on board with the graduation WIG. But soon other departments wanted in on the action.

Chris, the head of the human resources department, approached President Leslie one day and said, "My team is very upset with you. When you set the WIG to increase graduate rates, we said to ourselves, 'We're in H.R., we never even see students. How can we possibly contribute?' You didn't think to include us." Chris was right; Leslie hadn't thought about them at all in relation to the WIG. "But we figured it out," said Chris triumphantly.

"We realized we had critical information about careers and salaries. We know what people earn. We don't want students to be disappointed with their careers and compensation. So, we set a WIG to meet with a handful of students. We ended up with several hundred students in the session, then thousands. We have had such meaningful success with so many, it has opened up our perspective so that we really contribute to the student graduation rate!"

The human resources department helped raise the graduation rate by advising students early on about their career prospects. As students made more informed decisions about a major, the graduation rate increased. Of course, information on careers and compensation had always been available, but no one was focusing on getting that information to each student.

Chris the H.R. Manager told President Leslie, "Don't limit your staff to only their jobs. Open up the opportunity to do the *real* job to be done, which is the organizational WIG. Make sure you see the potential in every team and person. It takes the entire organization to create graduates—everyone from the facilities people to the human resources people to the faculty."

And that's how the Alamo College District got every one of thousands of faculty and students on board and aligned to the same WIG. And their results, which we will share more of later in this book, were spectacular, eventually earning them the prestigious Malcolm Baldridge award in 2018, the only community college ever to receive the honor. If they can get aligned with that many pieces in play, so too can a large and complicated K-12 district or a single school facing many difficulties.

Use this tool to align WIGs across the organization:

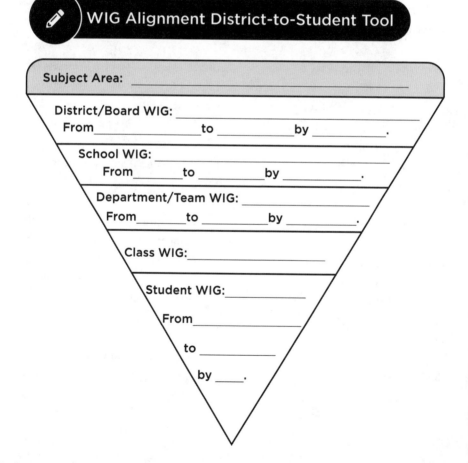

WIG Alignment District-to-Student Tool

Subject Area: _____

District/Board WIG: _____
  From_____to _____by _____.

School WIG: _____
  From_____to _____by _____.

Department/Team WIG: _____
  From_____to _____by _____.

Class WIG:_____

Student WIG:_____

From_____

to _____

by _____.

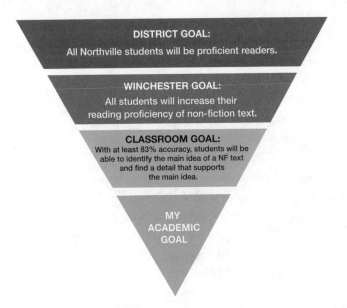

DISTRICT GOAL:
All Northville students will be proficient readers.

WINCHESTER GOAL:
All students will increase their
reading proficiency of non-fiction text.

CLASSROOM GOAL:
With at least 83% accuracy, students will be
able to identify the main idea of a NF text
and find a detail that supports
the main idea.

MY
ACADEMIC
GOAL

You can see how Northville Public Schools use this alignment tool to ensure that there is a clear line of sight from the District's WIG all the way to the Student's WIG.

Collaborate on choosing WIGs. Of course, a leader is ultimately responsible for the success of a WIG. That said, when people expected to carry out the WIG are included in choosing the WIG, they "own" the WIG and are more motivated to execute it. If it's just the choice of the principal, dean, or superintendent, the executors are less likely to commit to it. Furthermore, leaders are wise to leverage the knowledge of those people when formulating the WIG.

As a leader, we like to say that you can veto but not dictate what the WIG should be. If, for example, you are the principal of the school and you're trying to decide on a single school WIG, involve your other key administrators and some or all of your teachers. Work together to identify some candidate WIGs. You may even feel very strongly about what you think that WIG should be, which is fine, but please don't ever dictate what the WIG will be. Of course, if the team comes up with a WIG you don't agree with, you have the right, as the leader of the school, to veto that suggestion. That's why we say, "you can veto, but don't dictate."

What if the WIG is handed down from above? It's true that a WIG might be imposed on you, but more often you'll be asked to align your

WIGs with those of your leaders. For example, as a principal you may have no choice about the goals the district has set. But you do have a choice to select a WIG of your own for your school that is aligned to the District goals. In education, we often say "design down, but deliver up." Outcomes might be defined and handed down, but the way you deliver those outcomes is usually up to you.

Define From X to Y by When. We measure success on a WIG this way: From X to Y by When. Every WIG at every level must contain a clearly measurable result, as well as the date by which that result must be achieved. For example, a school WIG might be: "Increase the number of students reading on grade level from 45% to 65% by May 25." Identify where you are today, where you want to be, and the date for reaching that destination. A WIG always needs a start line (From X), a finish line (to Y), and a deadline (by When).

✎ **From X to Y by When Tool**

_____ will go

from [instruction level] _____

to [instruction level] _____

by _____.

Suppose we take Karl's goals and define them in terms of From X to Y by When. Which of these columns makes the clearest statement of the goals?

GOAL	FROM X TO Y BY WHEN
As a school we will improve our mathematics summative assessment scores.	Increase the average mathematics summative assessment score from 72% to 80% by January.
Narrow achievement gaps across racial and economic lines.	Increase the average GPA of socio-economic minority students from 2.2 to 2.8 by the end of year 2.
Do character education to improve school citizenship values.	Decrease the average number of monthly suspensions from 15 to 5 by the end of the school year.

The goals that Karl was so proud of were literally unfulfillable because there was no From X to Y by When. One of his goals was "Ensure all students become knowledgeable, responsible, caring, and contributing members of society." How would he measure success on such a far-reaching goal? How could he even establish a starting line? What kind of finish line could he possibly have in mind? It's an unactionable goal; yet we constantly run into objectives like this in Strategic Improvement Plans.

Where do you get your From X to Y by When? Of course, schools have different success measures. Some schools administer an annual survey from an accrediting organization. Others measure school performance by looking at data about leadership development, school culture, and academic results.

As deceptively simple as the formula may seem, many leaders often struggle to translate their school improvement goals into the formula From X to Y by When. Of course, some goals are easier to measure than others. For example, if your WIG is a project, like building a new media center, it's easy to tell when it starts and ends. But if your WIG is to improve the character of the students, you'll want to explore many possible ways to define From X to Y by When and get some consensus on what the measures mean.

If a goal is to be wildly important, surely you should be able to tell if you've achieved it or not. The formula From X to Y by When makes that possible.

WIG in Action: Shooting for the Moon

In 1958, the fledgling National Aeronautics and Space Administration (NASA) had many important goals like this one: "The expansion of human knowledge of phenomena in the atmosphere and space." Their goals sounded like many of the goals you hear in education today: "Every student will achieve at such and such a level..." NASA's goals lacked clarity. They also lacked the results that the Soviet Union was achieving.

But in 1961, President John F. Kennedy shook NASA to its foundation when he challenged them to "land a man on the moon and return him safely to the earth before this decade is out." Suddenly, NASA had a Wildly Important Goal, defined in exactly the way WIGs should be defined: "X" was earthbound, "Y" was to the moon and back, and "When" was by December 31, 1969.

Just a glance at this table shows the difference between NASA's conventional goals and a true WIG.

SOME OF NASA'S GOALS IN 1958	NASA'S GOAL IN 1961
"The expansion of human knowledge and phenomena in the atmosphere and space."	"I believe that this nation should commit itself to achieving the goal, before this decade is out, of landing a man on the moon and returning him safely to earth."
"The improvement of the usefulness, performance, safety, and efficiency of aeronautical and space vehicles."	—John F. Kennedy
"The establishment of long-range studies of the potential benefits to be gained from, the opportunities for, and the problems involved in the utilization of aeronautical and space activities for peaceful and scientific purposes."	
"The preservation of the role of the United States as a leader in aeronautical and space science and technology and in the application thereof to the conduct of peaceful activities within and outside the atmosphere."	
"Cooperation by the United States with other nations and groups of nations in space activities and in the peaceful application of the results thereof."	
"The most effective utilization of the scientific and engineering resources of the United States, with close cooperation among all interested agencies in order to avoid unnecessary duplication of effort, facilities, and equipment."	

Consider the 1958 goals:

- Are they clear and measurable?
- How many are there?
- Is there a starting line, finish line, or deadline for any of them?

How compelling were NASA'S 1958 goals? What kind of results were they getting? Russia went into space first with satellites and cosmonauts while the United States was still blowing up rockets on launchpads.

Contrast the 1958 goals with the 1961 goal: One clear, measurable WIG.

Now, with its reputation at stake on the world stage, NASA had to determine the few key actions that would achieve that lofty challenge. Consider just how lofty it was! They would have to fly through space at 18 miles per second to a precise location on the moon, which was orbiting rapidly around the earth. No rocket heavy enough to carry a lunar module had never yet achieved a velocity sufficient to break free of Earth's gravitational pull. They also had to develop a spacecraft that would keep astronauts alive while traveling to and from the moon and exploring its surface.

President Kennedy's WIG also required saying "no" to many other worthy goals. "Why, some say, the moon? Why choose this as our goal?" he asked. His answer: "That goal will serve to organize and measure the best of our energies and skills, because that challenge is one that we are willing to accept, one we are unwilling to postpone, and one which we intend to win."

Looking back on history, it seems remarkable that Kennedy might have faced some opposition to this goal—but he did. Not everyone bought into the goal, and some powerful people pushed back. According to a tape recording of a White House meeting of November 21, 1962, NASA Administrator James Webb questioned the priority of the lunar-landing goal, asserting that the United States space program had many other equally important priorities.

Kennedy responded, "This is, whether we like it or not, a race. Everything we do [in space] ought to be tied into getting to the moon ahead of the Russians." Kennedy told Webb that winning the moon race "is the top priority of the agency and except for defense, the top priority of the

United States government."[10] Kennedy would not back down. He narrowed NASA's focus to one WIG, and they responded eagerly.

What do you think happened to accountability inside NASA when the moon project was announced? It went through the roof. What happened to morale and engagement? It, too, went through the roof. Most leaders find this surprising. We tend to think that when people are held strictly accountable, morale goes down. The reality is this: Narrowing your focus increases both the accountability and the engagement of your instructional team as well as your students.

When a team moves from having a dozen "wouldn't-it-be-nice" goals to one or two "no-matter-what" goals, the effect on morale is dramatic. It's as though in everyone's head there's a switch labeled "Game on!" If you can throw that switch, you've started an engine of extraordinary execution. When President Kennedy said, "To the moon and back by the end of the decade," he threw that switch.

Despite those who said it was an impossible thing to do, astronauts walked on the moon on July 21, 1969. Looking back, we are astounded by that achievement. When you realize that the lunar spacecraft had only a tiny fraction of the computing power of the smartphone in your pocket, you might say that human beings had no business being on the moon in 1969.

Remember that the principle of focus is unforgiving. At some point, you will want to cheat on this principle, even just a little. We know. We often want to do the same. However, we've learned that the principle of focus is like the law of gravity: It isn't concerned with what we think. It operates independently of our opinions.

As we've said, the principle of focusing on the vital few goals is common sense; it's just not common practice.

Team vs. Individual WIGs

A team without a goal is not a team. You can't refer to your students or your faculty or your district staff as a team unless they have a common goal. A group of people with no common goal is just a group of people; but once you define a WIG, you usually need a team to achieve it. Obviously, John F. Kennedy wasn't going to the moon himself; literally thousands of people joined the team to bring about that WIG. Many teams had WIGs aligned to the big WIG. The WIG for the navigation team was to help the astronauts find the moon. The WIG for the propulsion team was to get the astronauts away from the earth and back again. The WIG for the life-support team was to keep the astronauts alive.

The WIG defines the team, not the other way around.

Did individuals on those teams have their own personal WIGs? No doubt. Mathematician Katherine Johnson had the WIG of calculating correctly the route the astronauts would take to the moon. Astronomer Ewen Whitaker had the WIG of pinpointing the best place to land on the moon. Although these experts relied on the support of others, their WIG was their job.

Can students have individual WIGS? Absolutely.

In many schools, teachers help students select and track progress on their own personal WIGs. For example, at Martin Petitjean School, each student has a "Leadership Notebook" for recording WIGs. For a while, the student's WIG might be to reach a certain score on a reading assessment; once that WIG is reached, the next WIG might have to do with math achievement. The WIGs are individually tailored to the student—a little stretch goal although still well within the student's capacity.

Individual student WIGs should align to the classroom WIG, which in turn aligns to the school WIG. For example, as illustrated earlier, one of Martin Petitjean's WIGs was 97 percent attendance every day. One day before school started, a mother called Dr. Cummins, the principal, to explain about her son Jon, who was about to begin the first grade. "He is sickly," she said, "and extremely shy. Going to school gives him stomach aches. He missed 45 days in kindergarten. He's probably going to miss a lot of school."

"Well, you can't miss 45 days!" thought Dr. Cummins. But once Jon got into school and learned about the attendance WIG and how important it was to everyone, he began to make a real effort. The first semester, he missed only ten days—a definite improvement from kindergarten. "At our school, the students lead parent-teacher conferences, and I asked if I could sit in on Jon's conference," Dr. Cummins says. "He did an astounding job presenting his leadership notebook to his mom. Later, his teacher explained to me that Jon had chosen a personal WIG to learn to speak in front of people so he could read aloud in church on Sundays."

For students, we usually recommend that they have an academic WIG aligned to their classroom WIG and also have a personal WIG. A personal WIG doesn't have to align to the classroom WIG—it's something wildly important to the student, as in Jon's case.

He had done such an incredible job of reaching his personal WIG that the school recruited him to be master of ceremonies at the school assemblies. He also made the announcements over the intercom for the students every day. He was the one who got to announce that the school had won an award for near perfect attendance.

Through second and third grade, Jon himself racked up a perfect attendance record. Then in fourth grade he got sick with the flu. "He wrote me a letter to explain that his doctor had ordered him to stay home," says Dr. Cummins. "So, he missed a week of school, but he wanted me to know that it wasn't his fault!" Jon's personal WIG transformed his life—from a shy boy who was sick at the thought of facing other people, to a self-confident young man with great skill at presenting himself in public.

Examples of Schools with Wildly Important Goals

Below are three examples of setting a Wildly Important Goal, one from a district and two from individual schools. Although we don't yet know the outcomes of these WIGs because they were put in place at the time we were writing this book, we anticipate that the focus these WIGs provide will lead to great outcomes.

Closing an Achievement Gap. For a long time, the Board of Education of Des Moines Public Schools in Iowa had been concerned about the less advantaged children in the community. As in many American urban school districts, an academic achievement gap persisted due to racial and socio-economic inequities. They decided it was past time to give their finest energy and focus to closing that gap.

First, the Board of Education boldly acknowledged the system of supports, or lack thereof, were at the root of the underperformance of black males in the district. The data showed an unmistakable gap. Then, instead of papering over the problem with vague aspirational rhetoric, they adopted three specific and Wildly Important Goals aligned to their core beliefs about equity and social justice.

WIG 1: The percent of all third grade students on track in reading will increase from 52% to 72% by June 20—using the Formative Assessment System for Teachers (FAST).

WIG 2: The percent of black, male third grade students on track in reading will increase from 35% to 72% by June 20—as measured by FAST.

WIG 3: The percent of black, male students earning a 'B' or higher in Algebra 1 by the end of ninth grade will increase from 17% to 35% by August 20.

By getting extremely specific about the WIGs, the Des Moines district could say no—"pleasantly and smilingly"—to other good ideas that could distract from their efforts. According to Associate Superintendent Matt Smith, "[This focus] creates a dynamic North Star. All of our metrics are in service of these Board goals."

Changing a Culture. The massive organizational change in Des Moines did not happen overnight. Matt knew it would take time for 4DX to gain traction in a district that serves more than 31,000 students. He compared the Des Moines initiative to a shot of Novocain—"You know it's going to work, but you have to allow time for it to take shape and form." The district launched 4DX through the Talent Support Department, the group in charge of staff development. Because they already had a supportive relationship with the staff, this group could help install 4DX in a non-threatening way across the district.

To demonstrate that all departments were valued, the district rolled out 4DX beyond just the academic staff. For example, the central office manages construction, custodians, facilities, food preparation, printing, technology, and buses that log more than 1.6 million miles each year. Every department was challenged to develop WIGs and measures for serving children better and aligning to the board's goals.

At the department-head level, about 25 goals were identified the first year. The next step was to narrow them to a few WIGs. The process fostered an understanding of what each team was doing instead of finger-pointing and expounding on what others *thought* they should be doing. It took time to overcome a "silo" mindset within the various departments.

We had unintentionally perpetuated silos in our district. The silos are where racism goes to thrive, where sexism goes to thrive. Because you're not accountable to anybody. You don't allow anybody into your space, in your heart, your spirit, your mind, or in your processes that exist in your in your department, in your area of influence.

The 4DX process, he adds, "demands an environment where you open your closet and allow yourself to be vulnerable and to grow in your leadership style." Matt says it helped develop the mindset of "us in service to one another in supporting students and families."

Today, Wildly Important Goals are present and visible across the district in the board room, offices, and classrooms. All departments—not just the schools—are collecting data daily to inform their progress toward WIGs. They roll the data up to the central office, where they evaluate whether they're winning or making no progress. They decide who needs more or less support based on actual data. "Real-time support at the student level—that's the ultimate vision here," says Matt Smith.

Changing the culture of an entire metropolitan school district was a major achievement. 4DX was the catalyst to make it happen. Of course, every school has its own culture, and cultural change at the school level can be daunting as well. The administrators at Sager Elementary School (not the real name) found that bullying was rampant in the upper grades. The principal had no doubt that an intimidating atmosphere was not only affecting academic performance but also hurting children physically—there were lots of absences, stomach pains, and headaches.

A survey of the students shocked him. Nearly 50 percent of the older children reported that they had been bullied, and seven out of ten said they had seen bullying occur at the school. The alarmed staff wanted to reduce bullying reports to zero, but they worried their expectations for cultural change might be too high. So, they settled on this WIG:

WIG: Reduce reports of bullying from 50% of students to 25% by the end of the school year.

Although the principal had many priorities, he made this WIG top priority and focused on it in meetings with parents, teachers, police officers, community leaders, and the students themselves. Soon, everyone in the Sager School community was involved in the campaign—even the bullies started to take note.

Changing Behavior. At a middle school in California, fitness suddenly took priority when an external study revealed that nearly half the students were obese, far more than the already high 20 percent in the rest of the state. Administrators were startled to find that students spent only a few minutes in vigorous physical activity even during Physical Education classes. The children risked diabetes and heart disease in later life; furthermore, other studies showed that physically fit children improved their academic performance by six percent.

In consultation with parents and district medical staff, the principal and staff proposed a WIG:

WIG: *Students will go from 5 minutes of "Moderate-to-Vigorous Physical Activity" (MVPA) to 60 minutes per day by the end of 9 months.*

Moderate-to-Vigorous Physical Activity, or MVPA for short, gets your heart beating faster and your breathing heavier. For kids, MVPA might include riding a bike or a brisk walk. Doctors recommend that teens get at least an hour of MVPA per day.

Practicing Discipline 1: Focus on the Wildly Important

Let's summarize the process for practicing Discipline 1: Focus on the Wildly Important.

1. Select Wildly Important Goal(s) (WIGs) as a team. What gap is most worth closing? What is most critical to your success? What are the one or two things that require your best energies? What are the chief goals of your organization? Brainstorm freely, then rank candidate goals by impact. Select the top 3 or so to research and experiment with. Then select the one measure with the most impact.

WIG Finder Tool

BRAINSTORM WIGS	RANK	SELECT CANDIDATES	SELECT WIGS
Verb...			
Verb...			
Verb...			
Verb...			

2. Check your WIGs for alignment with the goals of your educational authorities. If there are misalignments, reconsider your WIGs in consultation with those authorities. For example, if your department is not clear on the WIGs of your instructional area at the district level, you need to get together with them and collaborate on WIGs that align.

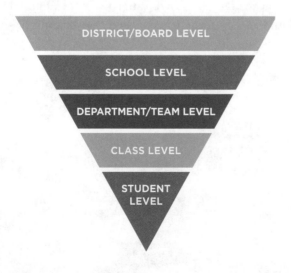

3. Determine From X to Y by When.

_____ **will go**

from [instruction level] _____

to [instruction level] _____

by _____ .

"X" is the current reality. What is the baseline according to your best data? For example, the percentage of students proficient on a given exam, the current GPA of the students in your school, the percentage of students enrolled in fine arts classes, and so on. Once you know the current reality, measure the gap by defining "Y."

"Y" is the future desired state. It might come from the government or the district or the principal. It might come from your professional association. Or it might be your own opinion of where you want to be.

Suppose you want to close a reading proficiency gap in your third grade. You can calculate the gap through a simple data-analysis formula. Group the students by proficiency. Using the formula below, calculate what your target should be.

Example:		N = Number of students assessed in our school/team/class
3rd grade reading		
		A = Number of students who "exceed standard"
N = 80		
		B = Number of students who "meet standard"
A = 10		
		C = Number of students who are "approaching standard"
B = 35		
		D = Number of students who are "well below standard"
C = 25		
D = 10		$\dfrac{A+B}{N} = X$
(10+35)/80=56		
(10+35+25)/80=88		$\dfrac{A+B+C}{N} = Y$

In this case, the WIG would read: "Raise third grade reading proficiency scores from 56% to 88% by June."

Using this data set, why do we leave the lowest 10 students out of the formula? It is simply for the purpose of calculating the "Y." We are not saying we should ignore these students. We expect all children to learn and grow and we will help all students to achieve. This is merely a way to calculate a realistic target or "Y."

Even though you still have to deal with the whirlwind and its myriad demands—attendance, professional development days, parent/teacher conferences, (besides teaching!)—you also have a finish line, something clear and important at which you can win. What's even more meaningful, each member of your team will know they are making an important difference. Everyone wants to feel they are contributing something of value; when times are tough, they want it even more. Discipline 1 enables you to move from concepts to well-defined targets, from a vague, strategic intent to a set of specific finish lines.

Discipline 1 also means narrowing your priorities down to one or two that are "wildly important." As one fourth grade student advised the principal of his school, "When you're meeting your goal, don't keep adding a bunch of stuff, because you won't really know what you're doing."

Imagine the simplicity of this class WIG:

TEACHER'S 4TH GRADE CLASS WIG

100% of our class will grow their scores on the reading assessment by the end of the term.

Every one of this teacher's students knows exactly what the target is. Everyone knows what matters most, which adds force and power to the goal. And their individual WIGs tell them exactly how much they need to grow:

STUDENT'S WIG

I will go from scoring 65 to scoring 75 on my reading assessment by the end of the term.

Other subjects and scores are also important, but the student knows that this one requires her finest and best effort. In the midst of her whirlwind, she holds tightly to this goal.

Finally, Discipline 1 means leaving a "wildly important" legacy. Without intense focus on the wildly important priority, you never step beyond the whirlwind and you risk having a career of uneven and unmemorable accomplishment. With intense focus on the wildly important, your efforts will shine brightly in the eyes of your students and yourself. Remember Principal Karl. He will never free himself entirely from the whirlwind. He doesn't want to. He loves getting to know the students, watching football practice, and listening to the choir. However, by focusing tightly on a few Wildly Important Goals, he frees himself from the nagging feeling that the school isn't improving and that all his grand plans are gathering dust on his office shelf. Now he knows that someday he will leave the job having made a significant, measurable difference.

A Wildly Important Goal (WIG) is a goal that can make that difference. Most organizations have too many goals and cannot accomplish them all with excellence. It's better to focus on a WIG that will have the most impact on improving your school. Remember these rules:

- Focus on no more than one to three WIGs at a time—preferably one.
- Align your WIGs to the WIGs of your leaders.
- Collaborate on choosing WIGs.
- Define From X to Y by When.

Reflection: Lynn Kosinski
Learning and Luck

Several years after the "meeting of shame," I became a principal and was charged with writing the very state-mandated School Improvement Plan I had completely dismissed at the beginning of my career. At the time, state-mandated test results were publicly reported, but they had not yet evolved into the political football they would later become.

I had learned from experience and would not let history repeat itself. Our terrific staff helped to create the plan, and everyone knew our focus areas for improvement. That said, we concentrated on helping students progress and grow into good citizens and not on micromanaging to the plan.

We didn't measure our value by end-of-year assessments, rather developing the whole child. As a staff, we enjoyed working together and modeling positive, fun-filled relationships for our students. It wasn't utopia and we had our share of challenges, but we collaborated to meet and solve them.

Fast forward almost a decade later, and the U.S. government would enact "No Child Left Behind" (NCLB), a law that held schools accountable for how and what students learned and penalized schools that didn't show improvement. I was about to find myself in the middle of the fray over these new requirements.

The demographics of our middle school were economically and ethnically diverse. Some wealthier students enjoyed living on or around the many beautiful lakes in the community, while others depended on public assistance. Of course, they all dealt with the never-ending high energy and stresses of adolescence. Our job was to help them learn while navigating this transitional time in their lives. As if that wasn't enough, we now needed to respond to the demands of NCLB.

When NCLB launched, the various states imposed reporting standards for things like attendance rates and standardized test scores. Failure to meet these Adequate Yearly Progress (AYP) measures would bring unpleasant consequences and tremendous anxiety to our staff. We all watched for the inevitable to occur: When would a school in our district appear on *The List*—the list of schools that fell short on AYP? It didn't take long—our middle school had the dubious honor of landing first on the list, which brought a flurry of worried phone calls.

Colleagues called: "How can I help?" "Glad it's you and not me!" Every level of central administration called: "You've got to get off this list." "Go get 'em!" "We're sending help." While we knew we had to comply—and create yet another two-year improvement plan, no one had a clear, concise, tried-and-true method to help us execute such a plan.

This is where a little bit of learning and whole lot of luck entered. Regrettably, I did not know about the 4 Disciplines of Execution back then, or my response to this situation would have been far more robust and the outcome more predictable.

Although we didn't call it a WIG, we set one: *To go from not meeting AYP to meeting AYP by the end of the school year*. This meant earning certain standardized scores. The staff was clear on our focus and the deadline. Moreover, we were all committed to reaching this important goal.

But how to get there? The district sent a few content experts to help analyze the data and develop a strategy. The staff was very involved in creating the plan and brainstorming ideas to move our lag measures (as we now call them). In the end, every department had a solid strategy for going forward.

And our scores improved! We made it off the list and celebrated. Why then, after all these years, do I consider us just lucky? Don't get me wrong—we had great minds creating the plan and I had a dedicated and determined staff. But we didn't really have an implementation *system*. We just crossed our fingers and hoped for the best.

So, notwithstanding the talent of the team, we got lucky. Now, by practicing Discipline 2: Act on Lead Measures, it's easy to move past being just lucky. We can now confidently predict the outcomes of our best efforts. So, let's go on.

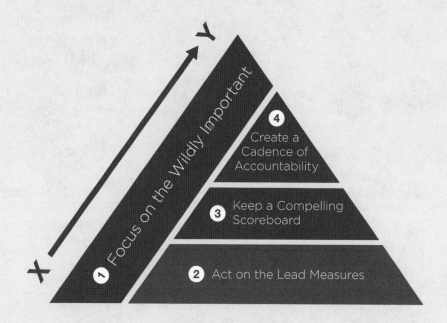

DISCIPLINE 2:
Act on the Lead Measures

Eighty percent of the results come from 20 percent of the activities.

When Bruce Leslie took over as president of the Alamo College system, the graduation rate was the lowest in the state of Texas—less than seven percent.

No one actually knew that until he started to dig into the numbers. When he told the faculty about it, they didn't even believe it. The shock led to some long, difficult discussions. "It was the first time we've ever talked about anything other than who had priority when classes were scheduled," Bruce recalls.

They worried about the dropout rate not only because of the financial hit to the colleges but also because of the thousands of students whose lives would be inhibited by a lack of education. Of course, it was a national problem. About 35 percent of college students across the United States never finish—but the Alamo problem was much, much worse than that.

So they set a WIG to increase the graduation rate. The "X" was seven percent; they chose a "Y" of a modest 10 percent for the first year. But how to get there? How to get dropouts to stay and finish? How to reach them and convince them graduation was worth the investment of time and money? And how to do it by the end of the school year?

At first, the leadership team felt somewhat helpless. But then they analyzed the data, disaggregating the students into cohorts based on their propensity to drop out of school. They discovered a few interesting details. For one thing, students who got college credit in high school (in an arrangement called "dual credit") were more likely to stay and graduate.

The dual credit program had always been there, but they had never focused much energy on it.

The team also discovered that students just didn't feel "at home" at the five community colleges. The Alamo colleges are commuter campuses. The students perceived the campuses as cold and impersonal by contrast to the feeling of belonging they had left behind at high school. Their loneliness combined with the stiff challenge of college work led many students to drop out.

The leadership team settled on two strategies for closing the From X to Y by When gap. They doubled down on recruitment for college-credit classes in the local high schools. They reasoned that more college-ready students would need less developmental education, thus freeing up dollars for other priorities.

They also instituted a new system-wide campaign called "Welcome Home!" The idea was to make every student feel that they belonged, that the campus was like home, and that someone there cared about them. "We changed our counseling system into an advising system," Bruce says. "Until then, the people in the counseling department stayed in their offices waiting for students to come to them for help. We took counselors out of their offices and into the classrooms where they could advise individual students in a proactive way. We hired a hundred new advisors and trained them as mentors and friends. Soon every student had an advisor, and every advisor had a cohort they were responsible for."

The "Welcome Home" theme soon pervaded the campuses, as staff were trained to pay attention to students instead of walking unseen past them. They would now say, "Hi, can I help you? Are you lost? What can I do to help?" There was a new feeling of belonging, not only for students but for staff as well.

And the numbers began to change. Alamo Colleges blew past seven percent; at the time of this writing, the graduation rate is around 26 percent—nearly a 400 percent increase in just a few years.

Lag Measures

As educators, we are inundated with data. Test scores, state evaluations, accreditation inputs, attendance figures, teacher ratings, safety incidents, financials, GPAs, crime statistics—the numbers go on forever. Additionally, a data trail now follows every student. We obsess over these numbers. Long administrative meetings are spent poring over data. The irony is, however, that no one really knows what to do with those numbers.

Why? Because they are all *lag measures*, so-called because by the time you see them, the performance that drove them has already passed. They are history. The whirlwind is full of lag measures. By the time you see the dropout numbers, for example, it's too late to do anything about them. A parent unhappy with her child's report card at the end of the term is helpless to change it. A state school superintendent who tremblingly opens the NAEP scores every other year is just as powerless as that parent. The reason people don't know what to do about lag measures is that no one *can* do anything about them. It's too late.

Still, lag measures are essential. In the context of the 4 Disciplines, lag measures track the success of your WIGs. The more precise the From X to Y by When, the better your lag measure. Without it, you would never know if you've succeeded or failed.

Bruce Leslie could have tried all kinds of things to get that lag measure. He could have campaigned, exhorted, expounded, and offered all kinds of incentives to students to stay; but in the end, he could only cross his fingers and hope.

What Bruce really needed were *lead measures*—the *critical* activities that lead to the lag measure. Where a lag measure tells you whether you have achieved your goal, a lead measure tells you *how* you will achieve your goal. Some people call these critical activities "strategies," others "key actions." We call them "lead measures."

Lead Measures

You can shoot for a big increase in your graduation rate, but you can't guarantee it. So, what can you guarantee? What you will *do* to bring it about.

You choose actions that will have the most impact on reaching the goal, and then track those actions. Those are your lead measures.

As educators, we worry about a lot of things: What will the government want next? What is technology going to do to schools? How do we get legislatures to invest more in education? What about the shortage of qualified teachers? Everything we worry about is in our "Circle of Concern." However, much of what we worry about is outside our control.

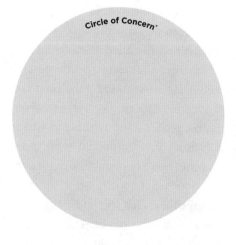

As Stephen R. Covey taught in *The 7 Habits of Highly Effective People*, we all have a Circle of Concern and we have no control over it. But inside that circle is another circle: The Circle of Influence. Within that circle are all the things we *can* control or at least *influence*, things such as our own behavior, our choices, our attitude, how we treat other people, and how we respond to whatever happens to us. Lead measures harness this principle, focusing our time and energy on what we can influence day to day, week to week, in reaching our WIG. By contrast, if we focus our time and energy on our Circle of Concern, we have less and less control over the WIG.

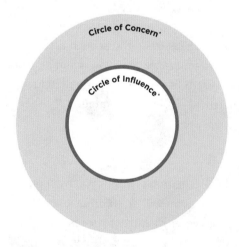

Bruce Leslie could not *guarantee* a higher graduation rate, but he *could* control what he did about it. Within his Circle of Influence were many actions he could take. The question was, which of those actions would have the most impact?

Discipline 2: Act on the Lead Measures is all about discovering those actions that will make the *biggest* difference in reaching your WIG—and then acting consistently on those lead measures. When you practice Discipline 1, you define a few Wildly Important Goals and a set of specific measurable targets. When you practice Discipline 2, you define the *strategies*—the behaviors or initiatives that will enable the team to achieve the WIGs. We call those strategies *lead measures.*

Discipline 2 is based on the principle of leverage—the axiom that some actions are more impactful than others. As you know, a lever amplifies your input to provide greater output: Given a big enough lever, as Archimedes said, "you can move the world." Like a lever, a lead measure is simply an action that is most likely to get the results you want. To get those results, you need to transcend conventional thinking about goals: Achieving your WIG is like trying to move a giant rock: you can put a lot of energy into it and still fail to move it. It's not a question of effort—if it were, you and your team would already have moved it. The problem is that effort alone isn't enough. The question is, do your efforts have enough *leverage*?

CONVENTIONAL THINKING	4DX THINKING
Keep your eye on the *lag* measures—the end-of-year results, the graduation rate, the summative assessments, etc. Stress out while you wait for the results.	Focus on moving the *lead* measures. These are the high-leverage actions you take to get the lag measures to move.

Consider the two primary characteristics of a lever: You control it, and it controls the rock. You can't influence the rock directly, but with a long enough lever you can predictably move the rock.

Once the Alamo leadership team learned about Discipline 2, instead of worrying about the things they could not control, they began to survey the range of things they could do that would have the most leverage on the graduation rate. They bet on two lead measures—dual-credit classes in high school and the "Welcome Home" campaign—to make a big difference to the lag measure.

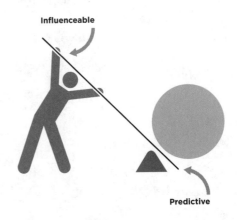

The lead measure is the lever that will move the big rock. So how do you find that lever?

When the staff at Seven Hills Elementary in Texas set a WIG to reach 90 percent reading proficiency within two years, they wondered what strategy to adopt to get there. Which of many possible lead measures would have the most leverage on the goal? After much data analysis and discussion, they came up with this: *Build teachers' capability and confidence through focused and aligned professional development.* From consultants at Teachers College, Columbia University they received coaching and mentoring. Teachers made commitments to try new techniques, and team members observed them. Together, they meticulously planned workshops, coaching sessions, and observations. Over time, the staff became measurably more "capable and confident" at teaching reading.

While WIGs can present themselves quite obviously in the form of achievement gaps, lead measures can be more challenging to identify. Teams need lead measures that are more than someone's good guess, and teams shouldn't settle for a strategy just because it's easy.

It takes discipline to discover lead measures. Identifying and acting on them becomes easier if you follow these rules:

Lead measures must be predictive and influenceable. Lead measures have two primary characteristics. First, a lead measure is *predictive*, meaning that if the lead measure changes, you can predict that the lag measure will also change. If it has leverage, it's predictive. Second, a lead measure is *influenceable*; it is within the team's control. That is, the team can make a lead measure happen without a significant dependence on any other factor; in other words, it's a lever you can move. The ideal lead measure is entirely within your "Circle of Influence."

LAG MEASURE	LEAD MEASURE
Measures output	Measures input
Easy to measure	Hard to measure
After the fact	Predictive: "Having the effect of producing a result"
Cannot be influenced because it's in the past	Influenceable: "Capable of being influenced or controlled"

To illustrate, let's take a WIG many people know about: losing weight. Obviously, the lag measure will be your weight loss as indicated by a scale. If you format this WIG correctly, you might define it as *Decrease total body weight from 190 to 175 pounds by May 30.* Easy to measure: just step on the scale.

Now, what are the lead measures that will be predictive of achieving the goal and, equally important, that you can influence? There are many possible lead measures, but let's say you choose the most obvious ones: diet and exercise.

The two measures fulfill the first characteristic of being predictive: Burn more calories than you take in, and you'll lose weight. Just as important, however, you can influence both measures. They are within your control. If you are otherwise healthy, the laws of physics dictate that less input and more output of calories will bring weight loss. Act on these two lead measures at the level specified, and you will see your lag measure moving when you step on the scale.

Lead measures must be tracked. If you're thinking something like "So, all you're saying is that if you want to lose weight, you should diet and exercise? What's revolutionary about that?" then you've missed the point of Discipline 2.

There's a huge difference between merely *understanding* the importance of diet and exercise and *measuring* your input and output of calories. Everyone knows they should diet and exercise, but the people who carefully track how many calories they've eaten and how many they've burned each day are the ones *actually* losing weight!

In the end, it's the *data* on lead measures that makes the difference.

A caution: diet and exercise are harder to measure than the number on the scale. When you eat that take-out dinner, you can usually only estimate how many calories you're consuming. And without the right equipment, it's hard to tell how many calories you burn when exercising. On top of that, regularly tracking lead measures is another chore. In sum, acting on lead measures requires consistent discipline. That's why we call this book the 4 Disciplines.

However, we believe strongly that acting on lead measures will be one of the most important insights you take from this book. We like to say that lead measures are where the magic happens. Your lead measures are your strategic bet, your best professional thinking about what drives the WIG. Over time, you will achieve your WIG in proportion to the investment you make in lead measures, as we have seen in many schools worldwide.

Let's look more closely at the characteristics of a good lead measure. Suppose your WIG is to *increase the average SAT score for the junior class from 1000 to 1100 by December 1*. The Y in the formula From X to Y by When is your lag measure. Your research shows that students do better if they attend weekend test prep classes, so going to these classes could be predictive of higher scores. However, you might have little influence over what the students do on the weekends. Unless you can provide excellent incentives, students might resist going to test-prep classes. Can you find a better lead measure that is both predictive *and* influenceable?

One of our colleagues, Breck England, did so when he was working as an eleventh grade English teacher. At the beginning of one school year, Breck gave his students a practice test and found that they averaged in the 38th percentile in reading, writing, and language. This score was not unusual; he had seen it over and over again for years. Furthermore, the students tended to show little improvement when it came time to take the Scholastic Aptitude Test (SAT) at the end of the school year.

Breck was tired of these mediocre results. In the United States, SAT scores can make a big difference in the lives of high school students. The scores often determine whether they qualify for scholarships and for the colleges they want to attend. Recognizing the importance of the SAT, Breck met with the principal and discussed the performance problem with parents. Eventually, he set a Wildly Important Goal for his students:

The class average on the reading, writing, and language section of a practice SAT will rise from the 38th percentile to the 90th percentile by April 30.

Closing a gap like this was a monumental challenge, and it was already October. Without the right lead measures, the goal would be not only unachievable but also demoralizing, so Breck carefully studied the original practice tests to find out exactly where students were falling short. Although there were problems everywhere, he noticed a pattern: The students consistently made errors of two kinds: punctuation and parallelism.

So, Breck drilled the students for weeks on these issues. Unfortunately, weekly quizzes demonstrated that the students weren't improving. What was the problem?

Gradually, it dawned on Breck that he was tracking lag measures, not lead measures. The end-of-week assessments were in practice no different from the end-of-year assessment. He was waiting till the end of each week to see if the drills made a difference.

He had mistaken lag measures for lead measures. Something else needed to be done.

Then he did something few teachers do: Instead of blaming the students for continually failing the quizzes, he asked them what *they* thought was wrong. Reluctantly, they told him they simply didn't understand *why* certain punctuation choices were incorrect. They had learned rules (for example, "Put a comma in front of a quotation") but didn't know the reasons for the rules.

After thinking about this, Breck chose another lead measure: *Teach basic grammar analysis daily so that students grasp the underlying reasons for punctuation rules.*

Starting with verbs, subjects, objects, modifiers, phrases, and clauses, he helped students build sentence structures from the ground up. Soon they began to understand why, for example, a compound sentence needs a comma and a coordinating conjunction. This work also helped them understand parallel structures.

It required hard work—mastering English grammar is not for the faint of heart—but eventually, Breck was satisfied things were turning around. He made adjustments based on his own reflections and the input of the students. Of course, many students resisted all this work, and he had to remind them repeatedly of the benefits to them. He also reviewed their progress with them weekly so they would understand the commitment he was asking of them.

Months went by. The last week of April, Breck administered the second practice SAT to the class. He knew that his students had leapt forward in their grasp of the subject, but he still held his breath while the machine calculated the scores. Excited, he announced the class average: 93rd percentile! His students were even more excited than he was.

After class, one student wandered back into the room. Breck noticed there were tears on his face. "I never thought I could do it," the boy said. "Every year I get a D in English. I know I'm not very smart, but I got an 88!" And an 88 percent on that test was more than respectable. The look of pride on that young boy's face meant more to Breck than anything else he had accomplished in his ten years of teaching.

It took some doing, but Breck had discovered a lead measure that would close the gap between X and Y. Teaching basic grammar turned out to make the biggest difference. It was both predictive and influenceable.

Lead measures require consistency in carrying them out. Once you've identified lead measures that are predictive and influenceable, you'll want to focus consistently on carrying them out.

In a way, you are doing a science experiment to see which measures have the most impact on your WIG, so it's important to keep a record of your lead measures, just as scientists do in a laboratory. For example, Breck would not have known his initial lead measure wasn't working if he hadn't regularly and frequently checked for progress.

Breck quizzed his students every week without fail. Of course, he had been doing those weekly assessments all along, but now he was using them to discern whether his lead measure was working. Like a doctor tracking a patient's progress, Breck shared the quiz results with the students and discussed what to do next. He involved them in making decisions. It was this consistent tracking of results on the lead measures that helped make the difference.

A lead measure might be a behavior you're already doing. After all, Breck was already teaching the rules of punctuation, but inconsistently and without intense focus. You might have a reading-improvement WIG and occasionally use reading intervention groups. You know they work well, but you haven't been consistent. So, your lead measure might be *Meet with groups three times a week*. Or your lead measure might be a behavior new to you, such as the "language-experience method." In any case, commit to making the behavior consistent and keeping track of your actions. Again, remember that you are going to need to put a disproportionate amount of time and energy on that key lead measure if you want to move the lag measure.

The leaders at Alamo College already accepted college credit for certain high school courses. They'd been doing it for years; however, they had never *concentrated* on it. They had never given it their full, intentional focus. By multiplying their effort, they managed to qualify and recruit many more graduation-bound students to their schools.

Lead measures also eliminate the element of surprise that a sole focus on lag measures can bring. Consider this scenario: You are at a carnival and you aim a water gun at a target to move your racehorse along a track against other competitors. You take aim and then close your eyes until the race is over. When you open your eyes, you are either excited you won or disappointed that you lost. But either way, there is nothing you can do to change the results. They are in the past. It's your lag measure.

Now, imagine playing the same game, only this time with your eyes open. Now you can constantly monitor your aim and the amount of water you are shooting at the target. The success of these two lead measures (aim and water) will have a direct impact on the lag measure (where your horse finishes in the race). You can predict along the way how the lag measure will change and the impact you're making.

Lead measures can be behavior-based or project-based. There are two types of lead measures: behavior-based and project-based.

Behavior-based lead measures track specific behaviors that you believe will lead to achieving the WIG. As noted, these behaviors might be new to you or things you're already doing but without focus and consistency.

Examples of lead measure behaviors might include teaching an extra block of remediation a certain number of times per week, implementing a certain number of differentiated reading lesson plans, or conducting extra vocabulary drills. Like a fitness coach, you help students carry out a certain number of exercises daily or weekly that are targeted at improving performance.

At one elementary school, a second grader was having problems with impulse control. For him, a lead measure was "complete two tasks each day from beginning to end." Tasks like "jumping rope in the hallway" and "watering plants" enabled him to work off some energy. Each time he completed a task, he would color in a square on a tracking sheet. As a result, he focused better on the task at hand and got better at controlling impulses to act out.

With a behavior-based lead measure, the team is accountable for performing the behavior, rather than producing a result.

Some examples? A school with a culture of bullying might adopt a lead measure of holding "restorative justice" workshops once a week where students encounter each other, discuss the harm done, and focus on ways to "restore" the relationship. If you have a passive group of foreign language students, your lead measure might be fifteen minutes of acting out scenarios in the language every day. In experimenting with lead measures, you are limited only by your imagination.

A *project-based* lead measure usually has a start and an end. It might be a research project, a professional development program, or an undertaking to build a new facility. For example, to close a student achievement gap in fractions, the team might choose to attend a workshop about strategies for teaching fractions. Or they might independently research methods for teaching fractions and then meet to come up with their own approach.

Breck's approach to his SAT-score goal mixed both approaches. His project was to teach grammar sequentially from the ground up, starting with parts of speech and arriving at complex sentence structures. He also included behavior measures. After evaluating their progress, students could choose three drills to do on their own time each week.

Both types of lead measures may be equally valid so long as they advance the WIG. Here are examples of the distinction between project-based and behavior-based lead measures:

WIG: **Increase monthly vocabulary assessment scores from 75% to 80% by January 31.**	
BEHAVIOR-BASED	**PROJECT-BASED**
Review 10 vocabulary words per week with my class through semester end.	Complete the Aardvark Affix Program online by end of first term.

WIG: **Adopt an online math curriculum by June 1.**	
BEHAVIOR-BASED	**PROJECT-BASED**
Spend 2 hours per week reviewing online math options.	Complete all project milestones by March 30.

When a team defines its lead measures, they are making a strategic bet. In a sense, they are saying, "We're betting that by focusing on these lead measures we are going to achieve our Wildly Important Goal." They believe that the lever is going to move the rock, and because of that belief, they engage.

Identify Your Lead Measures

Use this tool to select the lead measures for your WIG.

| WIG: _____ ||||
| LAG MEASURE: From _____ to _____ by _____. ||||
BRAINSTORM LEAD MEASURES	**P**	**I**	**SELECT CANDIDATES**	**SELECT LEAD MEASURE(S)**
Verb...				
Verb...				
Verb...				
Verb...				
Verb...				
Verb...				

1. Brainstorm together with your colleagues a list of candidate lead measures. Don't assume beforehand what they should be. Do not reject, criticize, or choose ideas prematurely. Listen carefully to each candidate. Start each idea with a verb. Why? Because a lead measure is an *action* you will take.

2. Rank the candidate lead measures from 1 (highest) to 10 in order of "Predictiveness" (P). Ask people to vote and explain their votes. Listen carefully to their reasoning.

3. Rank the candidate lead measures from 1 (highest) to 10 in order of "Influence-ability" (I) (in other words, which can you influence the most?). Ask people to vote and explain their votes. Listen carefully to their reasoning.

4. Select one or two candidate lead measures based on the group input and your personal judgment.

5. Experiment on these candidate lead measures. Carefully track your data and adjust your lead measures as needed.

Increase from 36% to 63% of students proficient on the NWEA reading assessment by June 1. That was the WIG for Edgemont Elementary School in Michigan. Data on the WIG was readily available; in fact, the assessment tool provided volumes of it, so much that the staff hardly knew what to focus on. They asked the same question we've heard from teachers around the world, "So what do we *do* to increase proficiency rates?"

We answered with a question "What do *you* think will help move the WIG?" They suggested a few ideas. Then we asked, "Which of these ideas would be most predictive and influenceable?" So, the team ranked each idea and selected three candidate lead measures.

Digging deeper, they examined sub-score measures and identified two reading categories showing the greatest need for improvement. For example, third grade teachers discovered that their students were having difficulty with vocabulary acquisition and use. That led to yet another question, "What is the test asking students to demonstrate?" Further analysis of the assessment showed the students struggled especially with affixes and Greek and Latin root words. Armed with this information, teachers were now ready to consider lead measures.

WIG: Increase student proficiency on the NWEA reading assessment. LAG MEASURE: From 36% to 63% by June 1.				
BRAINSTORM LEAD MEASURES	**P**	**I**	**SELECT CANDIDATES**	**SELECT LEAD MEASURE(S)**
Practice phonemics	3	3	Immediate positive feedback	Do focused instruction on affixes, Greek and Latin roots for 75 minutes per week.
Provide immediate positive feedback	2	2		
Use graphic organizers	4	5	Affixes, Greek and Latin roots	
Drill and focus on affixes, Greek and Latin roots	2	1		
Create mind-maps of texts	6	6	Sight-reading	
Focus on sight-reading	5	4		

They made the strategic bet that focusing daily on teaching specific kinds of vocabulary would move the lag measure. They tracked how often they did this and how the students were scoring on periodic quizzes.

Remember, this third grade team had lots of priorities to attend to. Like everyone else, they constantly battled the whirlwind of the day job; but once they followed the process for identifying a lead measure, they could focus on it with confidence that it would make the "wildly important difference" they wanted to make.

A common question: How do you choose the right lead measure(s) among all the candidates? How do you determine which candidate will provide the most leverage?

The answer: research and experimentation. Your aim is to find out as much as possible about the relationship between the WIG and your proposed lead measures.

In a way, discovering the right lead measures may be some of the most creative work you will ever do as an educator. You become a detective: you're getting to the bottom of the problem. You become a scientist: a researcher, an experimenter. The school is your lab. So how do scientists do their work?

1. Start with a hypothesis—a candidate lead measure. You should be able to predict reasonably well that it will have some effect on the goal.

2. Research. Look around you. Who else has achieved this goal or something like it? What did they do that was unique or different? What does the research literature say?

3. Analyze your data. Ask "why" questions about the data. For example, "Why are the third graders falling below the proficiency standard?" The data might show that half the students have "de-coding" problems—that is, they have trouble recognizing individual words. You should keep asking "why?" "Why the de-coding problem?" Soon you will arrive at a root cause you can address with a lead measure.

4. Select lead measure(s) based on your analysis. For example, you might focus more instruction on phonemics or word recognition to address a de-coding problem.

5. Record your results. Lead measure data is often more difficult to acquire than lag measure data, but you must commit to tracking progress on your lead measures. We often see teams struggling with this. "Recording all that data is just one more thing for us to do! We're too busy for that." Some feel micromanaged or overwhelmed. If that's you, we invite you to shift your paradigm on this. If you're serious about your WIG, then you must create a way to track your lead measures. Without data, you can't drive performance on the lead measures; without lead measures, you don't have leverage. And when the WIG is truly wildly important, you've got to have that leverage.

Finding the right lever among many possibilities is perhaps the toughest and most intriguing challenge for leaders trying to execute a

WIG. Lead measures are critically important to achieving your WIG. We implore you not to short circuit the time it takes to determine and vet appropriate lead measures.

As you select your lead measure or measures, remember the 80/20 rule, commonly known as the Pareto principle, which is that 80 percent of the outputs come from 20 percent of the inputs. Work to select those few lead measures that are the most leveraged and that will make all the difference. Then narrow them down to the fewest possible.

So, what if the lead measure you've chosen doesn't work?

Often, that means you've broken one of the rules above. If your lead measure seems inert and doesn't move the needle on the lag measure, ask yourself these questions:

- Is it really an "influenceable and predictive" measure, or did you choose something that was just "good to do"?

- Are you doing it consistently? Maybe it's a good lead measure, but you're not doing it enough.

- Are you doing it right? Maybe you're consistent, but not doing it well enough or precisely enough.

- Does it involve everyone? Sometimes leaders impose lead measures only they can do. For example, a principal might choose to give anti-bullying presentations to each class. That's nice, but are teachers and students also expected to take specific actions? Unless they're involved, they'll disengage pretty fast.

Of course, sometimes a lead measure just turns out to be ineffective, and you have to replace it with a new one. But don't give up. Lead measures are critically important to achieving your WIG. We implore you not to short circuit the time it takes to determine and vet appropriate lead measures.

Examples of Lead Measures

At Sager Elementary, the WIG was to reduce reports of bullying from 50 percent of the students to 25 percent. The staff saw this WIG as an important step toward changing a culture of intimidation at the school. Periodic surveys of the students showed a slight decline in bullying. But when the principal found a 10-year-old girl crying and bloodied on the school steps, he began having second thoughts about his lead measures.

He had done the obvious things: denounced bullying in speeches to the school and to the community, applied consequences to bullies when they were caught, and so forth. Clearly, however, stronger measures were needed.

The problem with bullies is that they are often hard to identify. Popular students who are otherwise well-behaved can turn into bullies when adults aren't watching. Too often accusations of bullying break down into "he-said-she-said" quarrels. The staff at Sager School brainstormed again on the problem and came up with an intriguing approach: Get the students themselves to police the bullies in their midst. The WIG was to reduce reports of bullying by half. These were the lead measures:

Lead measure 1: By December 1, all students in grades 5–7 will participate in five lessons about bullying and conflict resolution.

Lead measure 2: By December 1, all students will be able to name five strategies to address bullying as a victim or bystander.

Of course, this lead measure would not guarantee results, but it was predictive and influenceable. The staff made a strategic bet that intensive training on how to deal with bullies would change things. Experts came in to "teach the teachers." A curriculum was designed. The students learned "bystander strategies," such as how to defend a victim of bullying, to intervene effectively, to use humor to defuse a conflict, and to report a bullying incident.

Everyone in the school received the five lessons, which included a lot of modeling and role playing so students could rehearse what to do when confronted with bullying. The principal observed as many lessons as he could and gave feedback to the teachers.

Obviously, the staff had grappled with the bullying problem for years, but they had never given it consistent, concentrated attention like this. Now they had an ambitious WIG—to change the culture of the school—and they pursued the lead measure vigorously. By December 1, they had conducted 135 lessons on bullying across the school.

At a California middle school, the WIG was for each student to get to an hour of moderate-to-vigorous physical activity every day. Although there are many ways to get there, the school chose the easiest and cheapest way: just move. The lead measure was fairly easy to define:

Lead Measure: Students will run/walk 111 miles per month to reach 1,000 miles by the end of the school year.

Each student received a scorecard to track their miles per month. Some were walkers, some chose to run. The measure was ambitious, requiring about 75 minutes each day, and the students resisted (to say the least!) at first. But after a month they were enjoying the time together, and people got used to seeing them walking briskly around town.

Once a team is clear about the lead measures, their view of the goal changes. They get interested in tracking the data to see what happens. They begin to think of the 4 Disciplines as a game with a score—a game they can win.

This where the magic happens! Lead measures, when thoughtfully determined and executed, will make all the difference in reaching your Wildly Important Goal. Remember, lead measures are predictive of success and influenceable by you and your team.

Team vs. Individual Lead Measures

As we have said, the WIG defines the team. A schoolwide reading proficiency WIG might involve everyone, which means adopting one or two common lead measures. Then all the teachers at a certain grade level might have a team WIG that serves the schoolwide WIG. And then individual WIGs usually need individual lead measures; a particular student's reading WIG will require a lead measure tailored to that student.

To illustrate, a team of teachers assessed the students and sorted them into four categories: "exceeds standard, meets standard, approaches standard, and falls far from standard." (These categories were known only to the teachers.) Once students were assigned to a category, the teachers dug deeper to find out why students were performing at these levels. They identified areas of strength and areas for improvement. They then took the most significant delta within each group and did a root-cause analysis. From this analysis, they chose lead measures they could influence.

Here is a picture of one teacher's analysis. Across four areas (literature and information, foundational skills, language and writing, vocabulary use and functions), the teacher recorded each student's skill level. She wanted to discern patterns, so she color-coded each skill area. At a glance, you can see that foundational skills (yellow) were a strength for many students, regardless of achievement level; teachers knew then that they should put comparatively more energy into other areas.

		●	Δ
Literature + Informational L/I ~~(crossed out)~~			
Foundational skills FS			
Language and Writing L/W			
~~Vocab Use and Functions V/F~~			
A	Sammy	FS	
	Jeenna	L/W	~~L/I~~
	Hannah	FS	L/W
Exceeds	Gavin	FS	~~L/I~~ L/W
	Liam M.	L/I FS	L/W ~~L/I~~
	Lexi	FS L/W	~~L/I~~
	Xavier	FS ~~L/W~~	~~L/I~~ L/W
	Jayden P	~~L/I~~ ~~L/W~~	~~L/I~~ ~~L/W~~
	Liam S.	~~L/I~~	FS L/W ~~L/W~~
	Chace	FS	L/W
B	Jayden B.	FS ~~L/W~~	L/W
	Veda	FS	~~L/W~~
Meets	Matthew	FS	L/W
C	Brookelyn	~~L/W~~	FS
	A.J.	FS	~~L/I~~ L/W
Approaching	Jada	FS	L/W
	Max	~~L/W~~	L/W
	John	~~L/I~~ L/W	FS L/W
	Bella	L/W	
	Braxton	L/W	~~L/I~~ FS
D	Lilliana	FS	~~L/I~~
	Lukas	FS	~~L/I~~ ~~L/W~~
Far From	Ellie	L/W ~~L/W~~	~~L/I~~ FS

You can also see that the pattern of skills differed across groups. As a result, the teacher was able to choose lead measures that applied to the needs of each group. For example, the "D" group clearly needed more help with literature and information skills, while the "B" group did not.

This analysis also helped the teacher select lead measures for individual students. For example, Braxton is strong in language/writing but deficient in literature/information and foundational skills. Together, the teacher and Braxton set an improvement WIG and defined a lead measure to focus his energy on those deficits.

As a team, the teachers agreed on the following lead measures they would carry out together:

Lead measure 1: Meet with guided reading groups five times per week.

Lead measure 2: Teach a differentiated mini-lesson for each performance sub-group twice a week.

Most educators can tell you what lead measures will lead to achievement of a lag measure. At Highlands Elementary, teachers give their students a menu of lead measures, called a "pick list." Everything on the pick list is predictive and influenceable, as in this pick list of lead measures:

Lead Measure Pick List

Choose two lead measures from this pick list and paste them into the "My Lead Measures" boxes on page 1.

Use games for [*math/reading*] practice [___] minutes per day.

Use online apps/games [___] minutes per day.

Complete [___] task cards per day/week.

Use [*flashcards/manipulatives/letter tiles*] for [___] minutes per day.

Practice for [___] minutes per day with my Accountability Partner.

Meet with my teacher to practice [___] times per week.

Visit [___] learning stations per [*day/week*].

Record [___] videos or tutorials each week.

Complete a [*math/reading*] [*journal entry/graphic organizer*] [___] times per week.

If the WIG is targeted at reading proficiency, students can choose lead measures from a list like this one:

Example Pick List for Reading

READING	DEVELOPMENTAL LEVEL				SKILL GAP				WHERE IMPLEMENTED	
Lead-Measure Pick List for Students	Pre-K-2	3-5	6-8	9-12	Phonics Awareness	Fluency	Comprehension: Fiction	Comprehension: Exposition (Nonfiction)	Implement at Home	Implement at School
1. I will use my flash cards for X amount of minutes per day to match sounds to letters.	•				•				•	•
2. I will use my letter tiles for X amount of minutes per day to segment words into sounds.	•				•				•	•
3. I will do a word walk to identify sight words prior to reading.	•				•				•	•
4. I will read X amount of minutes per night.	•	•	•	•		•				•
5. I will complete and document two fluency touchpoints per week.		•	•		•				•	•
6. I will practice my weekly sight words for X minutes per day with my class Accountability Partner.	•	•			•				•	
7. I will read in unison with an adult for two minutes X times per week.	•	•			•				•	•
8. I will read to a student in my buddy class 15 minutes per week.	•	•			•				•	
9. X times a week, I will use a graphic organizer to respond to reading.		•	•	•			•	•	•	•

Students can pick from lists of lead measures the ones they think will help them achieve their WIG.

As students move into the upper grades, they become more independent about selecting lead measures of their own. "What do you think you should do on a regular basis to get to the goal?" the teacher asks. The student responds, "If I read with my parent for 20 minutes a day, it should help me get to the goal."

At Highlands, resource teachers give additional support to students who hesitate over the lead measures, but they can generally find some regular activity that connects to the goal. Acting on the lead measures builds confidence in the students that they can achieve the goal. As they believe in themselves more and more, their proficiency improves. As former principal Laura Mendicino says, "Confidence builds competence."

Some teachers might be part of a professional learning community with WIGs, or they might have their own individual WIGs. In any case, they should choose lead measures they can be relatively sure will lead to achievement of the WIG. Teachers might choose to improve their own skills by recording their instructional experiments in a journal each day. Members of a PLC might experiment together with instructional strategies like test-taking methods or small-group conferences. Here is a "pick list" of lead measures *Leader in Me* teachers have used.

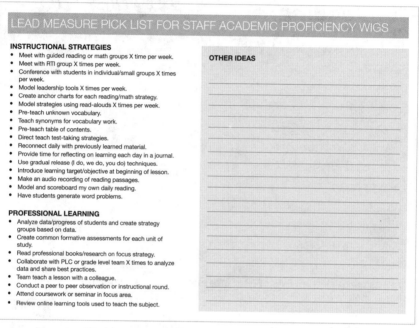

LEAD MEASURE PICK LIST FOR STAFF ACADEMIC PROFICIENCY WIGS

INSTRUCTIONAL STRATEGIES

- Meet with guided reading or math groups X time per week.
- Meet with RTI group X times per week.
- Conference with students in individual/small groups X times per week.
- Model leadership tools X times per week.
- Create anchor charts for each reading/math strategy.
- Model strategies using read-alouds X times per week.
- Pre-teach unknown vocabulary.
- Teach synonyms for vocabulary work.
- Pre-teach table of contents.
- Direct teach test-taking strategies.
- Reconnect daily with previously learned material.
- Provide time for reflecting on learning each day in a journal.
- Use gradual release (I do, we do, you do) techniques.
- Introduce learning target/objective at beginning of lesson.
- Make an audio recording of reading passages.
- Model and scoreboard my own daily reading.
- Have students generate word problems.

PROFESSIONAL LEARNING

- Analyze data/progress of students and create strategy groups based on data.
- Create common formative assessments for each unit of study.
- Read professional books/research on focus strategy.
- Collaborate with PLC or grade level team X times to analyze data and share best practices.
- Team teach a lesson with a colleague.
- Conduct a peer to peer observation or instructional round.
- Attend coursework or seminar in focus area.
- Review online learning tools used to teach the subject.

OTHER IDEAS

These are examples of lead measures that teachers have used for reaching both academic and personal/professional WIGs.

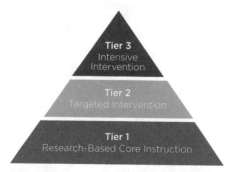

A Multi-Tiered Support System (MTSS) for students with varying skill levels might require different lead measures at each level.

Lead measures might vary depending on how intensive instruction needs to be to reach an educational WIG. In the USA, schools target support to students based on how much they struggle through a Multi-Tiered Support System (MTSS). To achieve the same WIG, lead measures might be selected for each of three tiers:

All students receive Tier 1 instruction, while Tiers 2 and 3 require more targeted or more intensive interventions. As a result, teachers might select from a pick list of differentiated lead measures for that tier.

While the process of identifying lead measures might seem labor intensive, resist the urge to short-circuit this important work. The stronger the data analysis, the more powerful the lead measures will be. To achieve a goal you've never achieved before, you must do things you've never done before. That's what lead measures are all about.

Practicing Discipline 2: Act on the Lead Measures

Discipline 2 is where the magic happens! Lead measures, when thoughtfully determined and executed, will make all the difference in reaching your Wildly Important Goal. Remember, lead measures are predictive of success and influenceable by you and your team. Once you identify the lag measure for the WIG and the lead measures that will bring it about, you track both measures consistently on a scoreboard. We will find out about that in Discipline 3: Keep a Compelling Scoreboard.

How many lead measures should I have for a WIG, you may ask? Just as we learned in Discipline 1, if you have too many areas of focus you diffuse your ability to get things done. So it is with lead measures. You should have only a few. We usually recommend that you have one or two leads for each WIG, sometimes three. You have many other data points at your disposal, but narrow down your leads (that you will give disproportionate focus to) to the fewest number you need to achieve the WIG—and that is typically one, two, or three at the most. Also, you will see when we get to Discipline 3 that too many lead measures become impossible to scoreboard.

Let's summarize the process for practicing Discipline 2: Act on the Lead Measures.

1. Select lead measures as a team (or as an individual in the case of personal WIGs). Derive the measures from brainstorming, hypotheses, research, and/or data analysis.

2. Rank the candidate lead measures from 1 (highest) to 10 in order of "Predictiveness" (P) (in other words, which is the most predictive?). Ask people to vote and explain their votes. Listen carefully to their reasoning.

3. Rank the candidate lead measures from 1 (highest) to 10 in order of "Influence-ability" (I) (in other words, which can you influence the most?). Ask people to vote and explain their votes. Listen carefully to their reasoning.

4. Select one, two, or three candidate lead measures based on the group input and your personal judgment.

5. Experiment on these candidate lead measures. Carefully track your data and adjust your lead measures as needed.

6. Make sure you track lead measures consistently and frequently.

Identify Lead Measure Tool ✎

WIG: _____				
LAG MEASURE: From _____ **to** _____ **by** _____ .				
BRAINSTORM LEAD MEASURES	**P**	**I**	**SELECT CANDIDATES**	**SELECT LEAD MEASURE(S)**
Verb...				
Verb...				
Verb...				
Verb...				
Verb...				
Verb...				

Reflection: Lynn Kosinski
Data Wallpaper

To say it was an impressive transformation of a meeting room is likely a matter of opinion. Every inch of the cinderblock wall was freshly covered floor to ceiling with magnetic whiteboards that displayed the latest assessment data for each school, complete with colorful graphs. In my new role as Assistant Superintendent, I wanted to view up-to-date information on student achievement everywhere in the district— all in one place. We as a leadership team had committed to monitor results and support school leaders in closing performance gaps.

When our school principals entered the room for the first time, though, they were less than excited. They seemed threatened. "What's the purpose of this data?" they asked. "Why is it on display in this meeting room? What are you going to do with it?" We at the district office were a bit surprised by this reaction.

Every administrator was used to watching scores as they came in. It's how we did the job. We were on top of the data, nobody could deny that. We picked apart the reasons for this and that result on state achievement assessments. We debated the reasons for our reading proficiency scores. But the school principals were uneasy in that room—they felt like we were weaponizing the data, leaning on them to do something about the numbers when we ourselves didn't know what to do about them.

At the district administration office, meetings were held in the new data room on a regular basis. Some days it wasn't uncommon for me to be in the room multiple times per day for several hours. Then, on one such occasion, after about the fourth hour of meetings in that room, a colleague asked me what I planned to *do* about all the data that was posted.

"Good question," I thought. It was in that moment that I understood what I had done. I realized I had created more-or-less useless data wallpaper.

The graphs and charts we so painstakingly updated would change nothing. We were monitoring the wrong things. All we had were lag measures. None of the data would help us *move* those lag measures. We had no lead measures. We had nothing that could help us predict or even influence the lag measures. We were essentially crossing our fingers and hoping for the best. We were data rich, but our thinking about data was faulty.

As we later found to our embarrassment, that wasn't the only flaw in our thinking. In that colorful room with floor-to-ceiling data wallpaper, the way we were tracking the data was all wrong as well, as you will see in the next chapter—Discipline 3: Keep a Compelling Scoreboard.

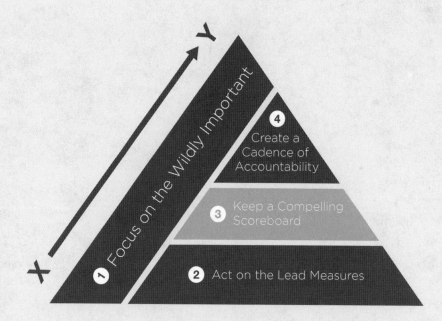

DISCIPLINE 3:
Keep a Compelling Scoreboard

People play differently when they're keeping score.

Imagine this scenario. In the distance is a group of teenagers playing soccer. You are far enough away that you can't hear them but you can see them. They are just kicking the ball around, tripping each other, having fun. One girl shows off a few long kicks, while a boy dribbles another ball aimlessly around, and yet another is practicing goal shots. Two girls are just talking on their phones.

Then things change. The kids form lines. Their play becomes strategic instead of random. They are really working at moving the ball and defending their goals. There is an explosion of energy on the soccer pitch.

What changed?

Obviously, they started playing *for real*. In other words, they began *keeping score*.

As long as no one is keeping score, people do what they want. There is little if any teaming. People do random things. Some are full of energy, some have little. Some work on their skills, some play, some just sit and chat.

But as soon as they start keeping score, they play the game differently. They team up, strategize, concentrate, and work hard, watching the scoreboard closely to see who's winning and how much time they have left. They are *engaged*.

Discipline 3: Keep a Compelling Scoreboard ensures that everyone knows the score at all times so they can tell if they're winning or not. When you practice Discipline 1, you define a few Wildly Important Goals and a set of specific measurable targets. When you practice Discipline 2, you define the lead measures that help you hit those targets. When you practice Discipline 3, you track and display the lead and lag measures of success on your WIG.

Discipline 3 is based on the principle of engagement—the axiom that the highest level of performance comes from people who are emotionally engaged. When they can see at a glance whether or not they are winning, they become profoundly engaged. They work with more purpose, ingenuity, and intensity when they are keeping score. By contrast, consider what would happen if the scoreboard disappeared from athletic competitions or elections. How quickly would everyone disengage? When would they stop caring about the outcome?

Teams that practice Discipline 3 translate their lead and lag measures into visible scoreboards that compel attention and action. Scoreboards help the team know where they are and where they should be. Without a scoreboard, energy dissipates, intensity lags, and the team goes back to "business as usual."

Our colleague Chris McChesney tells the story of a high school football game played in the American South. A windstorm had blown down the stadium scoreboard, but the game went on regardless. He recounts that it was a strange experience. The crowd of fans stopped watching the game and got caught up in other things. The play on the field became unfocused, haphazard. Clearly, when no one but the officials and the coaches knew the score, the heart went out of the game.

A team that knows the score works very differently from a team that only conceptually understands lead and lag measures. If the lead and lag measures are not captured on a visual scoreboard and updated regularly, the measures will disappear into the whirlwind. Simply put, people disengage when they don't know the score.

Many school systems are notorious for gathering mountains of data—grade distributions, attendance rates, benchmarks, course enrollments, assessment results, and more. However, most schools are "data rich but information poor"—they suffer from the well-known "DRIP syndrome." What does the flood of data actually mean? Education consultant Damian Cooper says, "The DRIP problem . . . is a curse of today's digital world. Because technology is so pervasive in our lives, so is data. When it comes to education, teachers and parents certainly don't suffer from a lack of data. The question is, how much of that data gets translated into useful information? And in this context, 'useful' means 'it helps improve learning.'[11]

Educators are not the only ones flooded with data. Parents and children try to keep their heads above the tides of data that hit them. Most of that data is in the form of lag measures, which show where students were on the day of the test but don't show how they got there.

What we're after in Discipline 3 is something quite different. In implementing Discipline 3, you need to build a "team scoreboard" designed solely to engage the team to win. To create a compelling scoreboard for a team, you need to transcend conventional thinking about the purpose of data:

CONVENTIONAL THINKING	4DX THINKING
Scoreboards are for the leaders. They are coaches' scoreboards that consist of complex spreadsheets with multiple data points. Their purpose is to enable coaches to strategize future moves.	*Scoreboards are for the team.* Team scoreboards are simple graphs or charts that show the current reality. At a glance, anyone can determine whether they are winning or losing. (An individual with a personal WIG should keep a personal scoreboard.)

It takes discipline to create a compelling scoreboard. It becomes easier if you follow these rules:

1. Scoreboards must be simple.

2. The team must be able to see the scoreboard.

3. Scoreboards should show both lag (From X to Y by When) and lead measures (start with a verb, show trends).

4. Team members must be able to tell immediately—within five seconds—if they are winning or losing.

5. Team members create and update the scoreboard themselves.

6. Personal data should not appear on public scoreboards.

Let's drill down on each of these rules.

1. Scoreboards must be simple.

The most compelling scoreboards contain only the information you need to see if you are achieving your WIG.

Here are two different scoreboards for the same soccer game. Note the lack of detail in the public scoreboard on the top. You see only the score and the time remaining in the period. That's all the fans and the team need—or want—to see. On the bottom is the coach's "stat sheet" that contains much more granular detail about the game. Here coaches track goals, assists, shots, percentage of shots that become goals, and so forth—data that will enable them to adjust their strategies.

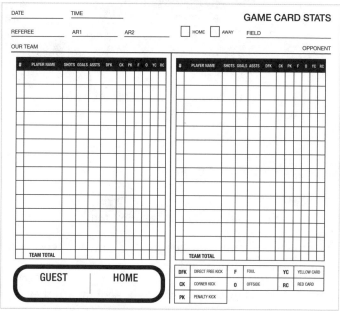

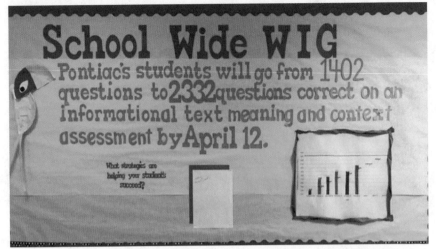

This scoreboard makes the school WIG so precise that no one could be in doubt about it.

As in this case, the ideal scoreboard makes the lag measure—the From X to Y by When—plain and unambiguous. It's a beautiful, Kennedy-style WIG: "To the moon and back by December 31, 1969." On April 12, everyone will know whether the WIG has been achieved or not. This kind of display adds urgency and intensity to the WIG. Note that progress toward the lag measure is charted in the lower right-hand corner.

For educators, a typical WIG is to demonstrate growth against a widely accepted standard, such as the NWEA (Northwest Evaluation Association) tests or the DRA (Developmental Reading Assessment). These assessments track student growth across the academic year so teachers can tell if their interventions are making a difference. In the sample scoreboard below, Savage Elementary has selected both these well-known standards as the lag measures for their WIG.

Of course, there's nothing new about NWEA, DRA, and other common measures. The Discipline 3 difference is that the school openly *focuses* on them and makes them *visible* to everyone; they are no longer hidden among many other measures in a leader scoreboard somewhere. And that takes us to the next rule of Discipline 3.

2. The team must be able to see their scoreboard.

The scoreboard in a big stadium is huge and the numbers are gigantic so everyone can glance at it to see how much time is left and who's winning. If your scoreboard sits on your computer or hangs on the back of your office door, it's out of sight, out of mind for the team. How can the team tell what to do if they can't see where they are?

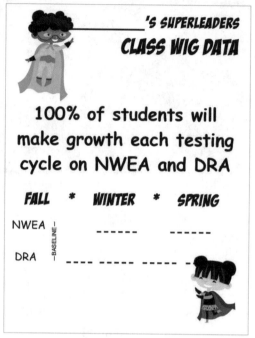

_____'S SUPERLEADERS

CLASS WIG DATA

100% of students will make growth each testing cycle on NWEA and DRA

FALL   *   WINTER   *   SPRING

NWEA

DRA

A quick look at this scoreboard tells you if students are improving.

Visibility also drives accountability. The results become personally important to the team when the scoreboard is displayed where everyone can see it. That said, exercise caution when scoreboards involve individual student performance data. Never display individual student data in a public place. It should be kept in a private location. In the United States and globally, we encourage you to comply with the rules for displaying data in the Family Educational Rights and Privacy Act (FERPA) and other student privacy regulations.

At Highlands Elementary, private scoreboards feed into public scoreboards. Principal Laura Mendicino says, "One of our lead measures is that every student should read 20 minutes a day. If they do, they get to color their square green. This creates a spirit of competition, especially if the class gets points for completing their lead measures. They can tell who's reading and who isn't, and it really changes their spirit. It's not a question of skill or shaming—it's simply a question of time. If you have a spare 20 minutes in class or a 20-minute ride on the bus, you can do your reading and then color your square green. Intriguingly, this practice not only helps close the achievement gap but also improves discipline. Students who are eager to get a green scoreboard aren't easily distracted from reading time."

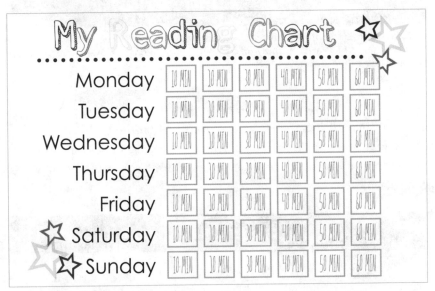

A simple individual scoreboard. Students color the squares green if they read 20 minutes a day. Once all students comply, they update their classroom scoreboard.

One of the most frustrating aspects of life in the whirlwind is that you don't feel like you're "winning." You might be giving everything you have to education, but you feel like you're just holding on for dear life. One value of a big public scoreboard is to showcase the wonderful progress your students are making. Visitors, parents, administrators, the media—anyone who comes to the school will be drawn to the imposing displays of student accomplishments, as in this school entrance hall:

At Hollywood Elementary, students in each grade show off their successes in this school. The "WIG World" display also provides staff a chance to explain WIGs to parents and other visitors.

Scoreboards excite everyone when they show dramatic progress, as in this display of increasing literacy measured on the DIBEL scale (Dynamic Indicators of Basic Early Literacy Skills). A public display of improvement builds confidence in students and the community that WIGs can be achieved!

	YEAR 1	YEAR 2	YEAR 3
First Grade	50%	58%	65%
Second Grade	40%	59%	80%
Third Grade	26%	53%	62%

Percentage of Improvement

When scoreboards are visible, even team members and students who have shown little interest in the WIGs become more engaged as they start to see that they're winning.

3. Scoreboards should show both lag and lead measures.

The lag measure shows the results we want to get, the lead measure shows how we plan to get there. The team needs to see both, or they will quickly lose interest. They need to see the cause-and-effect correlation of what they are doing (the lead), and what they are getting (the lag). Once the team sees the lag measure is moving because of the efforts they have made on the leads, they get more engaged.

This scoreboard shows both lag and lead measures so clearly that any observer can tell within a few seconds if this class is making progress or not. The lag measure is always written in terms of From X to Y by When. The lead measure tracks an activity that ensures the WIG will be met. It shows trends clearly from week to week. Each week the percentage of students who complete the activity is recorded, and the arrows indicate whether the percentages for that week are up or down.

4. **Team members must be able to tell immediately if they are winning or losing.**

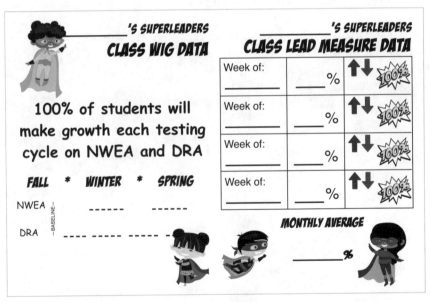

Ideally, a WIG scoreboard displays both the lag measures (left) and the lead measures (right), so that a quick look can tell you if you're "winning" or not.

At a glance, you can tell that bullying is decreasing at this school. You can also see that they are acting on the lead measure quite consistently.

LEAD MEASURE: Hold anti-bullying workshop each week of the term in each of the 12 grade levels.

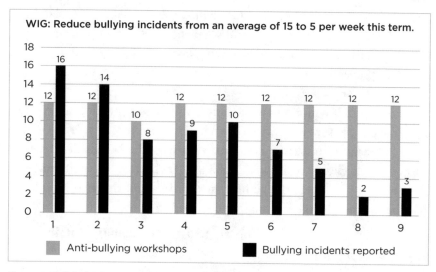

Can you tell in just a moment or two that bullying incidents are decreasing?

If the team can't quickly determine if they are winning or losing by looking at the scoreboard then it's not a game, it's just data. Glance at the grade distribution report below. Can you tell instantly who is winning or losing?

Grade Distribution by Teacher at AAA High School

Course Name	69	76	84	92	100	?	Total	Pass#	Fail#	Pass%	Fail%
1 English 1 Honors	1	1	5	8	9	0	24	23	1	95%	4%
2 English 1 CP	0	2	4	2	2	0	10	10	0	100%	0%
3 English 1 CP	1	5	1	2	1	0	10	9	1	90%	10%
1 Dual Enrollment English Comp.	0	0	0	0	0	0	0	0	0	0%	0%
1 Dual Enrollment Public Speaking	0	0	0	0	0	0	0	0	0	0%	0%
1 Instrumental Music: Jazz Band	0	0	0	5	10	0	15	15	0	100%	0%
1 ROTC Military Exhibition Drill	0	0	0	0	11	0	11	11	0	100%	0%
2 Chorus 1	1	4	7	13	11	0	36	35	1	97%	2%
1 Yearbook Production 2	0	0	0	2	2	0	4	4	0	100%	0%
2 Engish 2 CP	9	1	1	7	5	0	23	14	9	60%	39%
3 Engish 2 CP	6	2	1	6	8	0	23	17	6	73%	26%
1 Precalculus	0	0	0	1	13	0	14	14	0	100%	0%
2 Precalculus	0	1	1	1	12	0	15	15	0	100%	0%
4 Math for Technologies 2	4	6	3	1	1	0	15	11	4	73%	26%
2 Chemistery 2 CP	0	3	3	3	7	0	16	16	0	100%	0%
3 Chemistery 1 CP	1	5	2	9	9	0	26	25	1	96%	3%
9 Biology 1 CP	0	2	2	4	6	0	14	14	0	100%	0%
4 World Geography	4	1	6	6	6	0	23	19	4	82%	17%
5 World Geography	5	0	4	5	7	0	21	16	5	76%	23%
6 World Geography	1	2	9	5	3	0	20	19	1	95%	5%
1 African American Literature	1	0	3	5	8	0	17	16	1	94%	5%
3 English 3 CP	1	1	6	7	8	0	23	22	1	95%	4%
4 English 3 CP	2	0	1	5	14	0	22	20	2	90%	9%
1 Biology 2 CP	4	1	2	3	4	0	14	10	4	71%	28%
2 Physical Science CP	6	2	4	4	6	0	22	16	6	72%	27%
2 Biology 2 CP	4	0	3	7	3	0	17	13	4	76%	23%
1 Ed Plus 2	0	0	0	4	1	0	5	5	0	100%	0%
2 Ed Plus 2	0	0	1	2	3	0	6	6	0	100%	0%
4 Ed Plus 2	0	1	1	0	2	0	4	4	0	100%	0%
4 Math for Technologies 1	9	3	4	2	1	0	19	10	9	52%	47%
4 Geometry CP	0	7	3	6	4	0	20	20	0	100%	0%
5 Math for Technologies 1	9	3	3	3	3	0	21	12	9	57%	42%
3 US Hist. and Consti.	0	1	0	7	8	0	16	16	0	100%	0%
4 US Hist. and Consti.	0	1	3	3	16	0	23	23	0	100%	0%
5 US Hist. and Consti.	0	1	1	8	15	0	25	25	0	100%	0%
1 Math for Technologies 1	7	6	5	2	1	0	21	14	7	66%	33%
1 Prob. and Stat.	0	5	4	2	3	0	14	14	0	100%	0%
2 Prob. and Stat.	2	1	2	7	5	0	17	15	2	88%	11%
3 Physical Education 1	3	5	5	6	3	0	22	19	3	86%	13%
3 Teacher Assistance Program	0	0	0	0	2	0	2	2	0	100%	0%
4 Physical Education 1	0	0	2	11	8	0	21	21	0	100%	0%
4 Teacher Assistance Program	0	0	0	0	3	0	3	3	0	100%	0%
1 Web Page Design and Amp.	0	0	2	0	18	0	20	20	0	100%	0%
2 Web Page Design and Amp.	0	0	0	2	21	0	23	23	0	100%	0%
3 Web Page Design and Amp.	0	0	1	2	18	0	21	21	0	100%	0%

Although it is valuable for some purposes, this grade distribution report is not a Discipline 3 scoreboard.

Educators might use a report like this for many useful purposes, but not as a Discipline 3 scoreboard. If you can't tell within five seconds whether you're achieving the WIG or not, it's not a "compelling scoreboard."

Ideally, a scoreboard shows not only where you are on the path to the WIG but also where you should be, as this example does. The yellow line indicates the goal. You can see immediately that this team is making uneven progress. Ironically, they started out way above goal, but their performance has been fitful since then. You might interpret this chart in many ways, and all of those possibilities ought to be explored in accountability sessions, as we will see in Discipline 4.

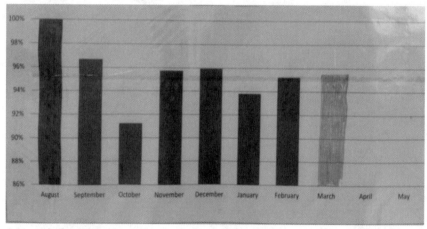

A record of achievement of lead measures. The yellow line shows where the team should be each month.

The scoreboard below shows how students are growing in reading from month to month. On the far left, the target has been visually represented. Each column shows how far they have left to go. Students can easily compare how they are doing against the target each month.

The scoreboard below meets the standard of a "compelling" scoreboard. In seconds you can tell what the WIG is and what progress the school is making toward the WIG. You can also see a correlation between the two lead measures and the lag measure.

WIG: MOVE FROM 450 TO 550 ON ASSESSMENT BY SCHOOL-YEAR END

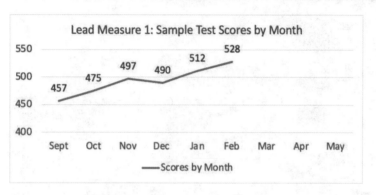

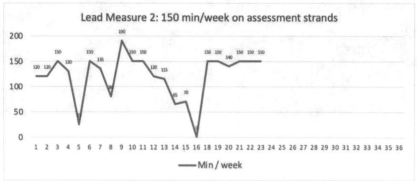

Note that the scores on sample tests correlate broadly to the amount of time spent in small groups studying the content. Clearly, these lead measures are moving the lag measure in the right direction.

Now, these numbers might have been available to the school for a long time. But once they are scoreboarded, the mental focus of the school changes. People get engaged in the WIG when they see the relationship between the lead and lag measures playing out on the scoreboard. It becomes a game for them. And once that "game on" switch is thrown, everything changes.

5. Team members create and update the scoreboard themselves.

We began this chapter with a critically important principle: People play differently when they are keeping score. Now, let's focus even more clearly on this principle: People play differently when *they* are keeping score. When team members *themselves* are updating the scoreboard, they truly understand the connection between their performance and their WIG and become more engaged in the goal.

Students themselves update their classroom scoreboards at Martin Petitjean Elementary School.

Students take real pride in showing off their progress to their parents and others. That's why a scoreboard of their own devising is more meaningful to them. In the sample below, the students have put it all together—the WIG, the lag and lead measures (which they call "strategies"), and the cadence of accountability (Discipline 4).

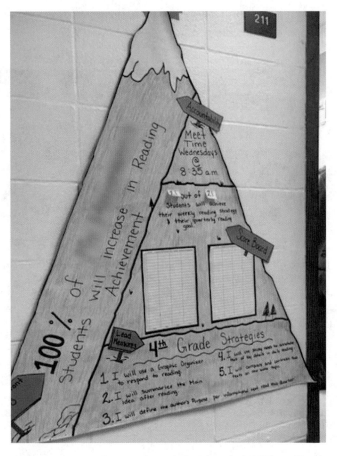

A fourth grade class created a scoreboard showing their WIG and lead measures, along with progress charts.

Scoreboards come in all shapes and sizes and can be kept at all levels of the organization. Principals can have a scoreboard—a dashboard if you will—that shows how teams are executing on their lead measures and how they are trending toward accomplishing the WIG. Teams and individual teachers can track their own metrics. And yes, students can track their lead and lag measures as well. Scoreboards can be useful at any of these levels.

Here is an example of a student's individual scoreboard. It shows her personal WIG—aligned with the classroom WIG—and the lead measures she will do to reach the WIG. Each day she colors in a circle to show she completed the lead measure for that day. At the end of a week, she reflects on her performance with "happy" or "sad" faces. Note also that she has a designated "Accountability Partner" and has planned a celebration for when she completes the WIG (see Discipline 4).

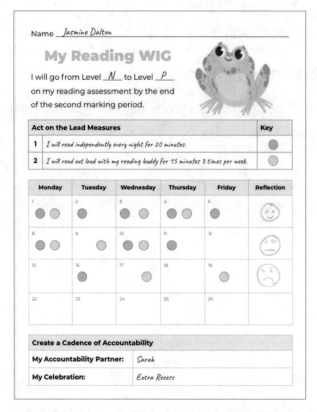

A simple scoreboard used by an individual student to track her performance on lead measures.

6. Personal data should not appear on public scoreboards.

Scoreboards may be public or private. The school may put a scoreboard in a public area, but it should never feature data that is private or personal. A public scoreboard might use line or bar graphs to demonstrate how the entire school is improving each quarter in its reading level WIG, but no individual student's reading performance should be visible.

Data relating to individuals should be on private scoreboards and kept in an area that's inaccessible to everyone but the team. Personal data must be kept private: it is unethical to display an individual's performance for all to see. Use these private scoreboards to measure the growth of small groups and individual students on scoreboards that might be color-coded by category: student, grade level, curriculum area, and so forth. These scoreboards allow the teams to discover patterns, collaborate to find solutions, and make every child visible.

Another reason not to display private data: Although it might motivate average or high-performing students, it can demotivate and even shame a student with challenges, resulting in a behavior problem. Most kids would rather be considered "naughty" than "dumb."

A classroom teacher may have both private scoreboards that show individual student progress and a more public classroom scoreboard that motivates students to accomplish the WIGs. Individual students use private notebooks to track their efforts. Many schools post private scoreboards in dedicated places such as team rooms and offices.

Here teachers can meet in private and discuss group performance as well as individual student progress.

In this example, teachers use a color code to determine if sub-groups (e.g., special education, second-language learners) are keeping pace with their peers.

Teachers use private scoreboards like this one to track individual student progress.

The teacher in the example below uses a private scoreboard to track her lead measure, which is to teach two grammar lessons per week. Two other teachers are conducting the same experiment; if it works, they will celebrate with a team dinner (why not add a little incentive to achieving the WIG?).

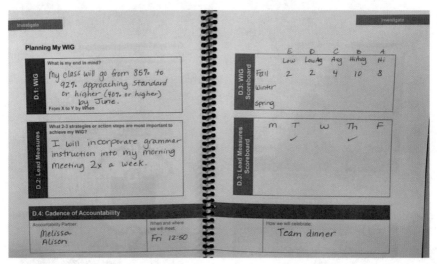

This teacher keeps a private record of her progress on lead measures.

Students should have private scoreboards of their progress on personal WIGs.

For even the youngest students, scoreboarding can help them successfully act on their lead measures. It helps to have WIG templates to record their activities. These fill-in-the-blank forms save time for teachers and ensure fidelity to Discipline 3. We've seen a lot of WIG trackers over the years. We've watched kindergarten students use bingo dabbers to record their work on a tracker that hangs on a cabinet in the classroom. The best ones are simple, like the template below.

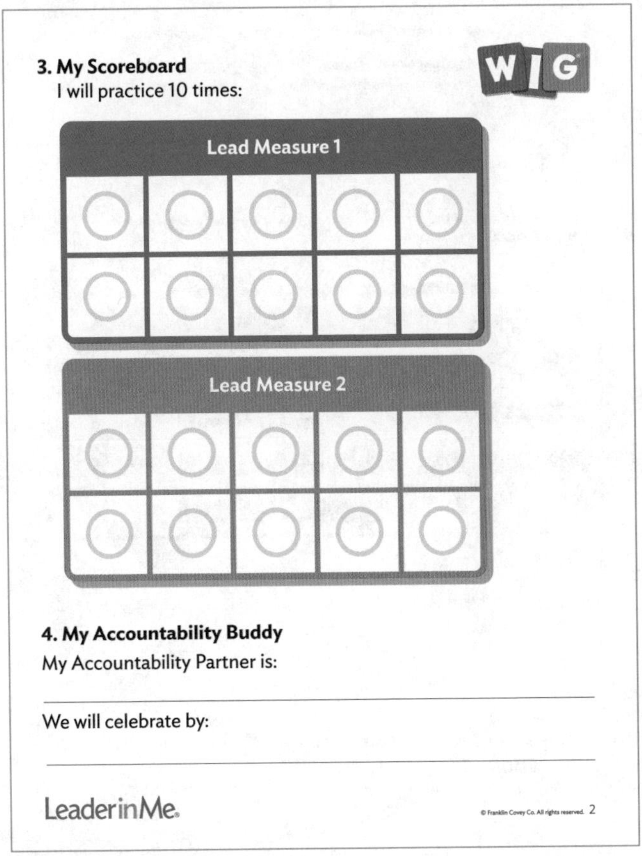

3. My Scoreboard
I will practice 10 times:

Lead Measure 1

Lead Measure 2

4. My Accountability Buddy
My Accountability Partner is:

We will celebrate by:

LeaderinMe.   2

On this simple scoreboard, students fill in a circle each time they complete a lead measure activity.

Young students might benefit from a template like the one below that puts everything in one place: the WIG, the lead measures, and a calendar of activities to fill in.

This individual scoreboard keeps students focused on the WIG and the lead-measure activities required to reach the WIG.

It also helps to have regular classroom routines for updating scoreboards. For example, if a student's lead measure is to complete an online lesson during the third period of the day, updating the scoreboard ought to be part of the activity.

Of course, individual students may also be encouraged to create their own scoreboards. This student's lead measure is to "read 7 sports articles a week" to improve his reading proficiency. Each week he colors in the space to show he has completed the task.

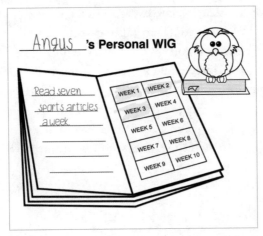

In another case, Jonathon was a boy who came from a challenging home life. School was way down on the list of priorities that included getting enough food to eat and a safe place to sleep. Now under state protection, Jonathon was back in school. He could read only 38 words a minute. The traumatized little boy needed some quick victories to build his confidence and ability to concentrate. Fortunately, his teacher helped him set an attainable WIG he could understand: To read 41 words per minute with accuracy by the end of the term.

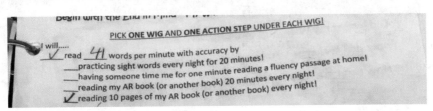

His teacher gave him a choice of lead measures, and he decided to read 10 pages of a book every night. This was an activity he could commit to. Within the term, Jonathan's teacher was stunned by the result: he went from 38 words per minute to 84 with 97 percent accuracy. She attributed his success to the motivation that came from fulfilling his action step and checking off his scoreboard every day.

Another boy named Jared also came from a difficult background. He and his little sister were foster children. Old enough to be in the third grade, Jared was about to go into special education because his reading skills were so far behind his age group. But an assessor noticed something odd about Jared—he often used big words like "buffoon."

The school felt that if Jared were motivated, he could leap quickly up to his age level for reading. In talking with him about his life, they learned that he worried about his little sister, who couldn't read at all. As they discussed goals, Jared came up with an unusual goal:

To teach my little sister how to read because reading is important.

Touched by this goal, Jared's teacher was determined to help him improve his own skills as far as possible. As Jared's scoreboard shows, they set a WIG to move him from first grade to third grade level by the end of the school year.

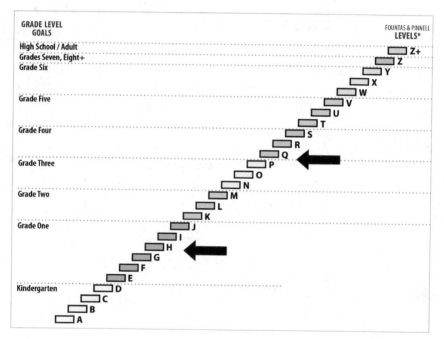

A personal WIG takes on definition when there is a scoreboard and a clear From X to Y by When.

For Jared, this would mean moving up seven reading levels by the end of the school year. And he achieved it. Over the ensuing months Jared worked on his lead measure of reading 10 pages of his Accelerated Reader (AR) book (or another book) every night, motivated by his goal of helping his sister learn to read. To make a long story short, he moved up seven reading levels and reached his goal.

As in Jared's case, when every student has a personal WIG and a compelling personal scoreboard, the "end in mind" becomes clear. Checking off the lead measures allows students to see their progress every day. As they do so, they become more confident and capable every day.

The purpose of a compelling scoreboard is to motivate, not to "name and shame" people. We have visited schools where they add a fuzzy ball to a big, clear tube every time a *collective* daily attendance goal is met. Kids are excited to watch the tube fill up and look forward with anticipation to the day it is completely full. This is fun and motivating for all!

But we've also visited schools where individual test scores are posted publicly and updated each quarter. In one school, each child has a car that moves along a track as he or she progresses in reading. Although the cars don't have the children's names on them, everyone knows who is out in front and who is lagging behind. One of the children told us, "I've been trying really hard, but that's my car way back there." He was so deflated! The scoreboard was compelling, all right—it was compelling discouragement!

A public scoreboard should not reflect individual levels of achievement. Instead, the public WIG should be that everyone makes measurable improvement.

NOT THIS	THIS
80% of students will achieve at least an 85% on the final exam.	All students will increase from their pre-assessment level to their post-assessment level by the end of the unit.

How would you feel if you were in the NOT THIS school? If you're a good student, you might think, "No problem. I can do that." However, if you're struggling you might quit trying as soon as that scoreboard goes up, knowing that it will be nearly impossible for you to get to an 85 percent on the final exam.

At Brookfield Academy Troy Campus, growth scoreboards are posted in the main hallway. They have incorporated the school mascot, the bee, into the theme of their scoreboards. The school WIG reads:

100% of Brookfield students will show growth on their math fluency assessments each quarter.

Note the lack of "X to Y." Individual students have their own "X to Y," so the school needs only to show that all students meet their individual lag measures. In this way, individual students are not shamed or embarrassed.

Brookfield tracks lead measures the same way. Thus, the lead measure statement is:

100% of Brookfield students will complete their lead measures every 3 weeks.

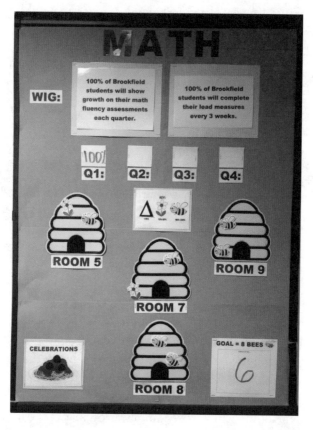

While students track their own lead measures daily, the data is collected at the school level every three weeks and a symbol is added to each hive representing the percentage of lead measures completed. If 90 percent to 100 percent are complete they earn a bee, 75 percent to 89 percent earns a flower, and less than 75 percent gets a delta. To encourage the whole school, once 8 bees are collected, they have a spaghetti celebration—not the kind where they *eat* spaghetti. The students get to slime the teachers with wet noodles!

While this public scoreboard keeps everyone up to date, the faculty monitors progress toward the WIG *privately*. Some teams keep electronic spreadsheets while others put up scoreboards on the wall, like the one below, for their own use.

This private team scoreboard is posted in a designated place away from students and the public. Note that the lag measure—From X to Y by When—is now posted, along with the lead measures. When the team gathers for their cadence of accountability meeting (see Discipline 4), they update the board so they can see if they are winning or losing.

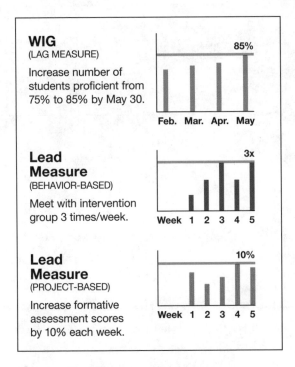

This faculty scoreboard contains the at-a-glance information the teachers need to gauge their progress toward the WIG.

To drill down to the student level, a more granular scoreboard can be helpful, as in the example below. At East Shore Leadership Academy, a colored magnet represents each grade level, and a numbered magnet represents each child. After each formal assessment, teachers take stock of the progress of the students, celebrate success, observe growth patterns, and plan their next interventions. The scoreboard tells them where they need to focus next.

K 44 4 26 / 1 23 5 / 2 6 / 3 7 / 8 9	F+P → PRE-READ	A–D K	E–J 1	K–M 2	N–P 3
NWEA-ELA ↓ Below 141	34 / 6 / 19	36 / 3 / 5 / 8			
141–159 (K)	27 20 / 39 / 41 / 1 / 12 / 14	22 30 38 10 15 / 23 31 40 26 17 / 24 32 42 36 18 / 25 33 43 2 21 / 28 35 44 8 / 29 37 9 16 / 2 7 11 13	10 71 / 11 / 15 36 / 16 34 / 18 16 / 22 / 26		
160–175 (1)		26 / 3 / 4 / 12 / 17 / 19	5 13 / 6 4 / 7 10 2 / 9 23 4 / 13 3 6 / 14 34 / 21 22	1 / 11 / 22 / 3 / 7	
175–188 (2)		26 / 24 / 27 / 15 / 13		1 52 / 3 35 / 12 57 / 13 41 / 14 5 / 18	11 30 / 14 / 11 / 13 / 19
188–198 (3)			15	4 / 7 / 9 / 28 / 17	2 34 / 4 / 4 / 7 / 9
198–205 (4)				14 34	14

The progress of individual students is tracked within grade level on this scoreboard.

Obviously, engaged people get results. But we know now, and have witnessed consistently over the years, that *results* also drive *engagement*. When students see themselves winning, they get more absorbed in the game. With the 4 Disciplines, you make a bet that well-defined lead measures will lead to a well-defined result. With Discipline 3, you are cheering each other on toward that result.

How to motivate students is an age-old problem. Think about how hard is to motivate *yourself*! If you're like most educators, you've probably been to meetings where they try to "psych you up" and inspire you to give your all. (Our experience is most educators are already giving their all.) But the compelling scoreboard can be more motivating than any program for psyching people up. Research shows that a person's ability to see a performance scoreboard "leads to increased ownership and sense of responsibility."[12] It's intrinsically motivating because it shows that you're winning, making progress, and advancing toward the WIG. When it doesn't, you have an opportunity to get back on track before it's too late.

The truth is, when people know what the goal is, know what to do about it, and know if they're winning or losing, it unlocks the best in them.

Practicing Discipline 3: Keep a Compelling Scoreboard

Let's summarize the process for practicing Discipline 3: Keep a Compelling Scoreboard.

1. Design scoreboards for each WIG. Schoolwide, classroom, personal/professional, student WIGs—they all require compelling scoreboards. Use a template or create your own.

2. Ensure that each scoreboard complies with these rules:

   - Scoreboards must be simple.
   - The team must be able to see the scoreboard.
   - Scoreboards should show both lag (From X to Y by When) and lead measures (start with a verb, show clear trends).
   - Team members must be able to tell immediately if they are winning or losing.

- Team members create and update the scoreboard themselves.
- Personal data should not appear on public scoreboards.

3. Update the scoreboard regularly.

Every scoreboard should contain the basic elements in the template below:

Sample Scoreboard Tool 🖊

WIG: Go from X to Y by _____.
(If possible, track progress from X to Y using a calendar, bar graph, line graph, pie chart, scatter gram, etc.)

Lead Measure 1: (Insert activity. Start with a verb.)
(Track activity using a calendar, bar graph, line graph, pie chart, scatter gram, etc.)

Lead Measure 2:

Lead Measure 3:

If the scoreboard doesn't motivate energetic action, it is not compelling enough to the players. All team members should be able to see the scoreboard and watch it change day by day or week by week. It should be at the forefront of their discussions as a team. They should never really take their minds off it.

Disciplines 1, 2, and 3 are powerful drivers of execution and yet they are really only the beginning of the story. The first three disciplines set up the game, but your team may still not be *in* the game, as you are about to learn in Discipline 4: Create a Cadence of Accountability.

Reflection: Lynn Kosinski
A Disconnect

After spending the better part of my career trying to crack the code on data analysis and closing achievement gaps, I thought we were making progress. As a leadership team we taught principals and teacher leaders a data-review process to train forward and implement at their respective schools. This process included reviewing assessment results and creating strategies to close student achievement gaps. Formally, the data review occurred on a quarterly basis. Informally, teachers met weekly in their Professional Learning Community (PLC) teams to discuss the progress students were making. It was a process that we felt had us focused, but it was not without its shortcomings.

While the system worked fairly well, there were still execution gaps. There was a disconnect between the quarterly data review, strategies determined, and the conversations in the weekly teacher PLC meetings. We did not have a quick and clear protocol for teachers to follow in order to report on commitments and share progress like you will learn about in the next section. Further, we lacked a system at the central office level to monitor the results that teams were getting at the various schools and grade levels, resulting in an unclear picture of school district progress as a whole. We were getting closer, but still searching for the lifeline I now know as the 4 Disciplines of Execution.

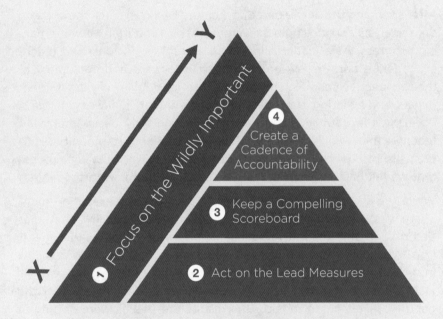

Y

X

1 Focus on the Wildly Important

4 Create a Cadence of Accountability

3 Keep a Compelling Scoreboard

2 Act on the Lead Measures

DISCIPLINE 4:
Create a Cadence of Accountability

Cadence: a regular, repeated, rhythmic pattern of activity.

As the new principal of Keswick Elementary, Wilma Williams was determined to turn around the school's academic performance. The state expected every school to reach 100 percent proficiency in key areas within three years; only 50 percent of Keswick students were proficient in reading and 68 percent in math. The school had barely made "adequate yearly progress" (AYP) the previous year. (AYP was a widely used measure at the time.)

Williams knew it would be tough to close that gap. Keswick was located in an area with a challenging demographic—two-thirds of the students were eligible for free or reduced lunch. Also, the school was structured to let students work "at their own pace"—a popular philosophy in some schools, but at Keswick it had caused many students to fall behind the expectations of the state. Worst of all, Williams found that the data used to reach AYP was misleading. The school had designated many students with reading problems as "disabled," thus excusing them from year-end testing. These students were not legally disabled—they merely had trouble reading.

So, the situation was worse than she'd thought. The school should never have achieved even "adequate" yearly progress. Accountability for results was not part of the culture at Keswick. Changing the belief system of the faculty and students would require time that she didn't have.

When asked about the AYP problem, everybody had their own causal story, an opinion often in the form of a narrative, to account for their performance. Eventually, though, Williams isolated "lack of focus, unaligned curriculum, lack of teamwork, and lack of data" as major issues she could influence.

As a first step toward "a culture of teacher accountability," Williams decided to implement benchmark reading tests aligned to state standards twice each term. Instead of holding the occasional faculty meeting devoted to administrivia, she met with small teams of teachers and focused on data. They would disaggregate data by student sub-groups to pinpoint students who needed the most help. "In every meeting I ask the teachers, 'What are you seeing in your benchmark testing?' We actually put student names in quartiles and track the student progress through the quartiles. So, we talk about data every time we meet." As they talked, lead measures surfaced in the form of activities they felt would help struggling quartiles. Reports of breakthroughs energized the small groups.

Soon students and staff were holding each other accountable for progress. Students were getting individual instruction. The frequent and regular team meetings—a "cadence of accountability"—was key to turning around Keswick's record of academic performance.[13] Although Wilma Williams was not familiar with the 4DX, her story shows the validity of the practice of regular and frequent accountability.

Discipline 4: A Cadence of Accountability

The fourth discipline is to create a cadence of accountability, a frequently recurring cycle of accounting of past performance and planning to move the score forward. As is self-evident in the name, the principle behind this fourth discipline is accountability, that we are all responsible to report what we commit to do and the results we achieve.

Educators often bristle at the word "accountability." It's been weaponized. Teachers get beaten up by parents and legislators and censorious media figures who are constantly pointing with alarm at "our failing schools." Holding educators "accountable" for this so-called "failure" has become a favorite theme of unsympathetic politicians.

Of course, most teachers already feel a deep sense of accountability for the performance of their students. They resent the imputation that they feel no responsibility for results. Most teachers welcome accountability. They want to tell their stories, but they have few opportunities to do so.

Administrators also feel the weight of rising expectations. "Since the task of leading a school has expanded and become more complex, the responsibilities placed on principals far exceed their capacity to handle them singlehandedly," says one educational scholar. "Though school leaders were traditionally only accountable for input into learning processes, they are now held accountable for all learning outcomes for both teachers and students."[14]

The traditional view of accountability is that administrators "hold people accountable." This mindset is often viewed as negative and controlling. But in the 4 Disciplines, accountability is positive. It's about a shared WIG. It's reporting exciting achievements. It's making personal commitments to help the team win. It's clearing the path for each other. It's about counting on each other.

This is the discipline that brings all the team members together to execute a shared WIG, and that is why it is at the top of the 4 Disciplines pyramid. To practice Discipline 4, we transcend conventional thinking about accountability:

CONVENTIONAL THINKING	4DX THINKING
• Accountability is "top down."	• Accountability is to each other.
• We're never quite sure what we are accountable for.	• We are crystal clear on our WIG and hold ourselves accountable for it.
• We get a performance review once a year, which everyone dreads.	• We meet every week to check on our progress and to help one another.

Conventionally, we might start the year with high-sounding goals and Strategic Improvement Plans. Then faculty members go off to their classrooms, shut the door, and try to do what they think is best. The whirlwind soon takes over, and the grand plans and goals are forgotten. In some schools, there's an annual performance review or a tenure review after five years, but many educators never get any input at all. And when reviews are held, school goals are rarely the focus.

By contrast, Discipline 4 focuses the school on a Wildly Important Goal. Educators never lose focus because all teams gather weekly to check scoreboards and decide together how to move the measures forward. These gatherings were Wilma Williams' primary tool for turning around Keswick Elementary School.

WIG Sessions

When practicing Discipline 4: Create a Cadence of Accountability, every team that is responsible for a WIG gathers regularly and frequently to evaluate progress on the WIG. This WIG session lasts no longer than twenty to thirty minutes in a weekly rhythm of accountability for driving progress toward the WIG. The agenda is simple:

1. Report on commitments you have made to "move the needle" on the scoreboard.

2. Review and update the scoreboard, celebrating successes and seeking to understand areas for improvement.

3. Make new commitments to move the measures even further.

WIG Session Agenda ✎

DATE:_____

Report on previous commitments:

Review and update scoreboards:

Make new commitments:

This discipline makes the difference between successful and failed execution. Let's look more closely at these agenda items.

1. **Report on commitments.** Each team member commits to certain activities that will "move the needle" on the scoreboard. Limit the discussion to those commitments. Questions to ask: "What did you commit to do last week to move the scoreboard? What were the results?"

   For example, the lead measure for a math department might require students to spend some time each week in the math lab. So, individual teachers might report on the efforts they made in the lab the previous week.

   Team members will be pleased to report that they have kept their commitments. They'll be even more pleased if it looks like their efforts have helped move the scoreboard. Those who haven't kept their commitments are accountable to the team. "Why not? What happened? How can we help?"

2. **Review the scoreboard.** Update the lead and lag measures. Questions to ask: "Are the measures moving in the right direction? Are we where we should be?"

   Celebrate successes and seek to understand failures. "Is our lead measure affecting the lag measure? If yes, why? What are we doing that's working? If not, what should we do? Do we have the right lead measures?"

   For example, "Each of us spent two hours in the math lab this week, but the lag measure didn't move. What ideas do we have now? Are we making best use of the math lab?" Or, "Our time in the math lab is paying off for some students and not others. Let's drill down and find out what's working and what isn't."

3. **Make new commitments.** Each team member commits to do something to move the measures this week. They apply lessons learned. "Okay, we found out that some of the students who are struggling the most are not coming to the lab. Let's try making appointments to meet them there personally."

If there are obstacles to keeping commitments, the team commits to clear the path of those obstacles. "Some of us have been assigned to work at the registration desk after school, making it impossible to work in the lab. What can we do to clear the path for them? Get them re-assigned? Change the lab hours? What else?"

You can see that the objective of the WIG session is simple: To hold each other accountable for your commitments to achieve the WIG despite the demands of the whirlwind.

Rules for the Cadence of Accountability

It takes discipline to keep the cadence of accountability going. It becomes easier if you follow these rules:

- Hold WIG sessions regularly and frequently.
- Make WIG sessions brief.
- Never allow the whirlwind into the WIG session.

Hold WIG Sessions Regularly and Frequently. The WIG Session needs to be regular. A "cadence" requires a regular rhythm. Without regularity, you'll lose focus quickly. Preferably, you should hold weekly WIG Sessions on the same day at the same time, as in the illustration below. Allow nothing to conflict with the WIG Session.

Note that "Collaborative Teams" (WIG sessions) are regularly scheduled at Chicot Elementary in Arkansas on Wednesdays.

Also, hold WIG Sessions frequently. Once a year may be "regular," but it isn't frequent. We have found that weekly sessions are about right for maintaining focus, although you might commit to meet more often or bi-weekly. Missing even a single week causes you to lose valuable momentum, and this loss of momentum impacts your results. This means that the WIG Session is sacred. This consistency is critical. Without it, your team will never be able to establish a sustained rhythm of performance. As one of our consultants says, "Commit or crumble."

"What's so special about holding a WIG Session each week?" you may ask. In our culture, a week embodies a perfect "slice of life." There's a natural rhythm of weeks in the academic calendar. We think in terms of weeks. Weeks have beginnings and endings. A week is short enough that you don't lose focus, but it's long enough for team members to keep their commitments.

Make WIG sessions brief. Twenty to thirty minutes at the most. Longer meetings tend to wander, and productivity suffers. Nobody likes long, aimless meetings. The WIG Session should be just the opposite: short and totally focused on the WIG.

"Another meeting?" you ask. "We don't have time for this." We hear you. Educators are on task every minute, teaching, grading, preparing, meeting with parents, supervising extra-curricular activities—even bathroom time is scheduled.

That's why WIG Sessions must be brief. But they are essential—that is, if the WIG is truly important and you really want to achieve it. We can assure you that you will not achieve it without a strict cadence of accountability. Life doesn't work that way.

Don't think of the WIG Session as a formal "meeting" around a big conference table. This is not the legislature or the United Nations. It's a quick, energetic update like a huddle of players on a football pitch. The WIG Session could be a "huddle in the hallway" where you review data on your tablets. Or you could hold your WIG Session via video conferencing. But there must be a regular cadence.

It's amazing what you can accomplish by the simple discipline of strategizing together each week about your goal. You might even start to think differently about time. As you move the needle on that most important goal, the WIG Session will become a "wildly important" time for you.

Never allow the whirlwind into the WIG Session. The WIG Session is not a faculty or department meeting. It is not a time to make announcements. It is not a time for "urgencies and emergencies." Resist the urge to complain about the mom who dropped in with birthday cupcakes at the end of the day, or the fire drill during the science experiment, or the fact that the state is going to demand changes to the curriculum *again*.

This kind of stuff will surely derail your WIG Session. No matter how demanding other priorities might seem, limit your WIG solely to reports and commitments to move the scoreboard. If you need to discuss other things, hold a staff meeting *right before* or *right after* the WIG Session, but keep the WIG Session separate.

The high level of focus makes the WIG Session not only quick, but extremely effective at producing the results you want. It also reaffirms the importance of the WIG to every team member. It sends a clear message that no success in the whirlwind can compensate for a failure to keep the commitments made in last week's WIG Session.

When Ty Handy took over as president of the Jefferson Community and Technical College, the school was $2 million in the red and losing students like crazy. When he read *The 4 Disciplines of Execution*, he realized how he could solve the crisis. Using 4DX, he focused the 85 teams at the college on student success measures as "wildly important." He included staff functions that are usually left out, such as facility management and housekeeping. "They now feel very tied into the mission of the college, which never happened before," he says.

Dr. Handy found the biggest challenge in implementing the 4 Disciplines was to get the cadence of accountability going in every department on all six campuses. But he was determined to make it happen because he understood the power of regular and frequent WIG Sessions:

"The cadence of accountability? It's the hardest piece to get in place, but *The 4 Disciplines of Execution* does the job. Most colleges know their goals, but they don't have anything in place to constantly focus their attention on them until there's a crisis. They'll ignore the data until they have to focus on it. The cadence—getting the focus on the goal into your daily routine—is what's missing in most schools. They think about the goal at the fall kickoff day or at the faculty development day each year. Maybe four or five days across the academic year they talk about how important the goal is, and then it's totally ignored the rest of the time. "

The results of Dr. Handy's dedication to his student success WIGs are impressive. "We have tripled the graduation rate of our underrepresented minority students. Our retention rate is up 10 percent, and everybody is talking about student success. The board says, 'This college is rolling on all cylinders.'"

Dr. Handy's persistence in promoting WIG Sessions continues to pay off; the college raised its graduation rate by more than 80 percent within three years. Likewise, Wilma Williams turned around a non-performing school and energized a stagnating culture through intense small-group meetings focused on data. We've seen the cadence of accountability transform schools everywhere.

Example of a WIG Session

We're listening in on the WIG Session of a Professional Learning Community focused on preparing students for college-entrance exams. Mai is the teacher-leader.

ANN: Thanks for being here. We're going to keep this session quick and energetic. The WIG is to get 10 percent more of our students into the 75th percentile, and we've got a little less than a year to do it. Let's start by reviewing last week's commitments.

JACK: Okay, I committed to evaluate the best online test preparation programs, and I've come up with three we ought to give a serious look.

MAI: I committed to research best practices for test preparation. A lot of the literature says that it's important for students to take at least two practice tests before the test date. That seems to be the best practice mentioned most often. There are several others to consider.

DIEP: We found out last week that the more reading the students do, the better they score. So, I've been studying ways to get more reading programs into the different departments. Most of the teachers agree with me, but I'm running into some resistance from the science and math departments. I could use some help.

TOMAS: We started the school year by encouraging more students to take challenging classes. We assumed that would help, and I think we're already seeing that assumption bear out. My commitment was to continue recruiting students for advanced placement classes, and I convinced three more students this week to try it. Not enough in my opinion.

ANN: Thanks for keeping your commitments, everyone. Let's look at the scoreboard and see how we're doing. Our first lead measure—encouraging enrollment in advanced placement courses—seems to be having an effect. This year we've seen a 20 percent growth in enrollment, and our latest assessments show about a five percent improvement across the school. Our second lead measure—encouraging reading across the curriculum—seems pretty static. What do you all think about that?

TOMAS: Too many students are still scared of accelerated courses, so they won't sign up.

JACK: What if we promised them they could get online help any time? I've researched one site that helps people practice for the test and offers live tutoring at a fairly good price. We'd have to work on the budget, but this program might help ease some fears.

ANN: I think we'd like to see a bigger improvement in those assessment scores, and anything that will help more students get into advanced placement—well, we need that.

TOMAS: I'd like to commit to get with Jack and evaluate that program this week.

JACK: That would be great. And you'd help me keep my commitment to choose the best online program, which I was planning to do this week. We're about ready to open the test preparation lab, so it's time to make a choice.

ANN: We'll put you down for those commitments. Now Diep has an issue with the science and math departments. How can we help clear the path for him?

MAI: They're set in their ways. We could get the principal involved, but that might make them even more resistant.

ANN: Let's brainstorm. Who has ideas for increasing the amount of science and math reading?

MAI: We could hold a contest for the best book report on a scientific subject.

JACK: The school already sponsors a science fair: Suppose we require that they have to bring at least two books to the fair that bear on their projects?

TOMAS: There's a comedy podcast about science that some of the kids like. We could have them listen to it in the test lab and answer questions about it. It's really funny.

ANN: These are all great ideas. Diep, could you commit to giving us a proposal by next week? Thanks.

MAI: The school book fair is this week. I thought I'd volunteer to help with it.

ANN: How would that help with our lead measures?

MAI: Well, I could promote science and math books and puzzles.

ANN: Great idea. Now, what about following up on best practices?

MAI: Yes, I need to do that. I'll need to talk to the English department about scheduling at least two practice tests before spring.

ANN: That'll work. Thanks everyone. We've had some good successes this week, and I think we ought to celebrate a little. The principal gave me some gift certificates for you all. And we'll be back here next week at the same time?

WIG Sessions Are Essential

From this example, you can see that WIG Sessions are not deep philosophical discussions, nor are they mechanical exercises. A WIG Session is a chance to look at the measures, check if what we're doing is keeping us on track, and decide what to do next. Like airplane pilots checking to see if they're on course, team members focus on the road ahead and the actions that will take them to their destination.

At Seven Hills Elementary in Texas, commitment to 4DX is extremely high. As we've seen, they had an aggressive WIG: *Our proficiency levels on literacy-based assessments will increase from baseline to 90% or greater by the end of the year.* Principal Kim Blackburn passionately applied the *4 Disciplines of Execution* in her quest to reach that lofty goal.

All the students set WIGS based on their individual needs—literacy goals, numeracy goals, and so forth. The students monitor their own progress toward the WIG by recording the lead-measure actions they take each day. Then, once a week, the teacher meets with them to evaluate how often and how well they are doing on their lead measures. Students who don't meet the weekly targets become priority for the whole campus leadership team. That team then does what they call a "WIG Walk" every Friday to determine how to support those students.

Kim knows that without a strong cadence of accountability for both students and staff, her proficiency goals would never be reached. This isn't just her opinion; she has data to prove the power of Discipline 4.

One lead measure at Seven Hills was to complete the lessons provided by a digital math program. Upon analyzing the data, Kim could see that post-assessment results across the school were mixed. Drilling deeper, she found that classes holding weekly "cadence sessions" were outperforming other classes by about seven percent. She followed up and found multiple data points that reinforced the value of Discipline 4 at the classroom level.

Over time, at Seven Hills, a strong cadence of accountability has been established. A private staff-only Professional Learning Community (PLC) room is the hub for faculty WIG Sessions. In this room they post the school WIG as well as grade level WIGs. Teachers gather there weekly in grade level teams to review their commitments. As teachers report out, a team member takes the lead and updates the scoreboard. The team follows a process based on a thinking tool (figure below), seeking to understand successes and failures.

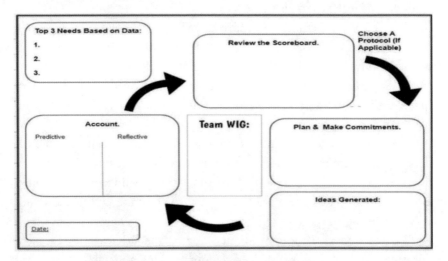

Thinking tool used in WIG sessions by staff at Seven Hills Elementary School, Texas.

They account for commitments they made last week and evaluate the predictive power of those commitments. They reflect on the actual results of keeping those commitments. Then they review the scoreboard, looking for patterns in the data that might suggest next steps. They generate ideas and make new commitments to test during the coming week.

Above all, they celebrate when they succeed. A true *esprit de corps* reigns in these meetings.

Kim says that weekly commitments make all the difference in achieving the goal. "Weekly commitments are things that the team should be doing naturally, but the reality is that these are the actions the whirlwind devours first. Without the steady rhythm of the WIG Session, there will always be things team members know they should do, but never do with real consistency." For Kim, the WIG Sessions provide the structure needed to reach the WIG.

The focus of the WIG Session is simple: To hold one another accountable for taking action to move lead measures, resulting in achievement of the WIG despite the whirlwind. Having this structure in place prevents the urgent, or the whirlwind, from entering into the conversation. The structure of the WIG Session helps us keep the main thing the main thing! What happens in the team WIG Sessions is that each team member realizes the importance of their commitment to the success of the *team*—and ultimately the school. It becomes personal! They begin asking themselves, "What can I do this week to move the lead measures?"

But the WIG Sessions are more than just mechanisms to achieve a goal. Kim is convinced that the constant focus and collaboration on wildly important priorities has changed the culture at Seven Hills Elementary. "WIG Sessions produce reliable results over and over again, but most importantly, what a good WIG Session does is produce a high-performing team."

Seven Hills teacher Marisa Goodwin found for herself that the cadence of accountability energized the culture of her classroom. At one point, the COVID-19 pandemic forced her class to do remote learning, and she wondered if she would have time to continue with the cadence upon returning to school:

"To be honest, I thought about skipping the WIG Sessions for the duration. With all the craziness of remote learning and such, I thought I could take it off my plate. But I quickly realized how flat my class seemed. There was no excitement and no camaraderie from working together as a class. The missing piece was our WIG Sessions, so I added them back into the schedule without hesitation."

One week she almost forgot to hold the WIG Session. "But then several students got excited and begged me to hold our WIG Session. Wow! Here I was so close to not doing it, but the kids are begging for it."

In contrast to Seven Hills, colleges have thousands of students across dozens of departments and a teaching staff numbering in the hundreds. The challenge there is to install and maintain a cadence of accountability that focuses on the overall college WIG of, for example, increasing the retention rate. In such a complex organization with so many lead measures, WIG Sessions keep that focus sharp. It takes numerous different commitments to move the needle on this WIG that involves so many entities.

Although the set of commitments becomes intricate, the basic principle still applies—each team member commits to do something to move the needle. Everyone stays fixated on the WIG, everyone works toward the same end, and every individual's contribution is valued.

Individual contributions are often made in the form of individual WIGs. How does Discipline 4 work for an individual? You might assign students to "Accountability Partners," another student or adult they can account to for progress on their individual measures. That person can help them define their WIGs and lead measures, track the scoreboard, and then meet with them in a cadence of accountability. Often, children are motivated more by their peers than by their teachers, so two or three students together can prompt a lot of progress as they report to each other. At one school they call their Accountability Partner, "accountabilibuddies."

The principle of the "cadence" creates habits of accountability that can serve students throughout their lives. At Highlands Elementary in rural Florida, about 40 percent of the students belong to migrant-worker families. The parents are in the fields from sun-up to sun-down, and when the seasons change, the families move. In October, the school saw an influx of hundreds of students, most of whom would then move north to plant the spring crops. So, almost half the year the students weren't even at Highlands.

"We see the goal of 4 Disciplines as lifelong success," says former principal Laura Mendicino. "Fortunately, the students learn the accountability system here, and then we encourage them to take it with them wherever they go." When they moved, students would take their goal trackers with them and continue to work on them. "One school in North Carolina called us and asked us to explain about WIGs. We told them about academic and personal WIGs and how to track lead measures. This school and others wanted to know all about our system because the students were self-starting. We told them that 4 Disciplines was a system for success for life."

"We had a third grade girl, one of our striving students, who was struggling with recognizing words. Her lead measure was phonics practice every day, and she could use our computer system to act on it. Then the family moved. Fortunately, the school she went to up north had the same system, so she was able to put in her twenty minutes a day—and we could see her progress! Soon she moved on from her phonics goal to a vocabulary goal. When she came back to us in the fall, her teacher came to me in tears, raving about the child's progress and how she had chosen to close her achievement gap herself. The little girl's ability to use the 4 Disciplines independently allowed her to press forward."

WIG Sessions Are for Celebrating!

Migrant children would come back to Highlands Elementary for a personal celebration of the goals they had met. Celebration of WIG achievement has become part of the culture at Highlands at every level: school, grade, classroom, and individual. Schoolwide success is recognized on the "WIG Wednesday Morning News," including grade level and classroom accomplishments.

Each week student and staff leaders go into a classroom for a little celebration with music. Students talk about the WIGs they have met, lead measures that were useful for them, and their next goals. Both academic and personal goals are recognized. "We called them up to the stage, one by one and by group. Group pictures, updated each week, hang on the 'Hall of Fame.' They get to sign their names on the pictures in the Hall of Fame and ring a 'WIG Bell.'

"We tried to move away from rewarding students with tangible items. We wanted that internal feeling of success to keep them going, that sense of accomplishment. We wanted them to know that they weren't always going to be handed a piece of candy," says Mendicino. Children are asked, "How does it make you feel that you reached that goal? Are you excited? Who do you want to go run and tell?" The principal would call parents to tell them their students have reached their goals. Instead of dreading a call from the principal, parents in that community learn to get excited when the principal calls. For students, WIG Sessions are not just accountability reports: they're like parties.

Seven Hills Elementary teacher Marisa Goodwin explains how she keeps WIG Sessions positive and motivating:

Our weekly classroom WIG Session always follows the same three steps: Each student accounts, reviews, and plans. Notice that I said "each student." It is the student who is making the commitments. I am simply a facilitator asking questions. "Were your commitments successful last week? What do we need to do differently this week? How can I help you?"

Because of this process, the WIG Session becomes positive and not punitive. This is crucial! The purpose is to motivate and engage rather than name and shame. We want students to have a growth mindset and know that they are contributing to the win even if they are not winning yet. I do not punish students for not meeting their goal. Instead, we look at students who meet their goal, discuss their strategies, and then make new commitments. This is true accountability. This is where culture is built. Students feel excited to be in the spotlight. They can see their contributions to the team. They then feel empowered to help others by offering suggestions or by asking for help.

The overall feel of the WIG Session is celebratory! This is the part that the students love and crave. Each week we celebrate students' progress. Every student knows that success is in their Circle of Control, so they are excited even if they don't meet their weekly goals.

With the weekly cadence, the students are highly motivated not only to meet their own commitments but to help everyone else meet their commitments. It's a weekly pep rally!

Finally, a classroom WIG Session shifts ownership of learning to the student, and because students feel in control of their goals, they are highly motivated. They want to work hard. They want to meet their goals. I don't have to tell kids to work at home. I don't ask kids to work at recess or lunch. They make those choices and are happy to do it! I had one student who was having trouble reaching his goal of 20 lessons. He said he wanted to work at home but kept forgetting. He asked if I could email his mom so she could help remind him, so I emailed mom explaining the situation. The student came back the next day, all smiles because he completed 4 lessons at home in one night! Here was a student excited to do homework! Have you ever heard of such a thing?

The WIG Session has tremendous motivational power when seen as a celebration. For example, at Alamo Colleges in Texas, President Bruce Leslie would bring the WIG teams to the meetings of the board of directors. "Everybody knew they could be called on any time to present to the board; so, if I had certain academic departments that were recalcitrant, I let them know they were going to present to the board, and to have fun with it."

Soon the teams were competing to impress the board with their presentations. The math department put on red, yellow, and white wigs. "It was so much fun. Departments came with Star Wars themes, Wizard of Oz themes, fashion themes."

The directors responded with wonderful affirmation. "Our teams loved showing what progress they were making, and the board gave them kudos. Soon, the first hour or two of every board meeting was all celebrations."

President Leslie also used these occasions to showcase the college to the community. "We brought in everyone we could think of to see these presentations. Everybody could see 'Here's what we've accomplished, here's where we have come from.'" At the Alamo Colleges, management doesn't have to demand accountability: Everyone is eager to account for their accomplishments in an atmosphere of celebration.

Here is a menu of ideas for celebrating WIG milestones at various levels:

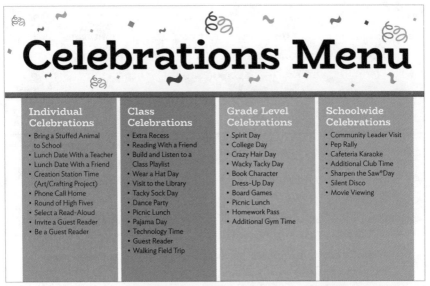

Celebrations Menu

Individual Celebrations	Class Celebrations	Grade Level Celebrations	Schoolwide Celebrations
• Bring a Stuffed Animal to School • Lunch Date With a Teacher • Lunch Date With a Friend • Creation Station Time (Art/Crafting Project) • Phone Call Home • Round of High Fives • Select a Read-Aloud • Invite a Guest Reader • Be a Guest Reader	• Extra Recess • Reading With a Friend • Build and Listen to a Class Playlist • Wear a Hat Day • Visit to the Library • Tacky Sock Day • Dance Party • Picnic Lunch • Pajama Day • Technology Time • Guest Reader • Walking Field Trip	• Spirit Day • College Day • Crazy Hair Day • Wacky Tacky Day • Book Character Dress-Up Day • Board Games • Picnic Lunch • Homework Pass • Additional Gym Time	• Community Leader Visit • Pep Rally • Cafeteria Karaoke • Additional Club Time • Sharpen the Saw® Day • Silent Disco • Movie Viewing

Here is a menu of ideas for celebrating WIG achievements, whether you're a kindergarten teacher or a college president.

Practicing Discipline 4: Create a Cadence of Accountability

WIG sessions might vary in content and complexity, but the agenda is always the same. Team members report on previous commitments, review and update the scoreboard, and make new commitments for the coming week. Here's the kind of language you should be hearing in the session:

DATE:_____

Report on previous commitments:

- I committed to meeting with my students two additional times this week. I did, and here's what I learned ..."

- "I committed to reading a book about online teaching methods. I didn't start it yet and here's why..."

- "I committed to trying exit slips to get feedback from my students, and this is how it went..."

Review and update scoreboards:

- "We're trending upward on our lead measures, but our lag measure for reading isn't moving. Maybe we need to re-think the lead measures ..."

- "Our lag measure is showing growth, but we have a challenge with our master schedule that could impact our ability to implement our lead measures..."

- "Lab 2 is making real progress on the assessments. We need to dig down and find out what they're doing differently..."

Make new commitments and clear the path for others:

- "Based on the data, I commit to raise my student contacts from two to three this week..."

- "I'll make sure to collaborate with the superintendent on a new schedule so you can keep your commitments..."

- "I can clear the path to the data you need. I am meeting with the Data Team on Thursday..."

Once a regular meeting cadence is established and a consistent agenda is followed, you will be surprised how much progress can be made toward carrying out lead measures with fidelity.

Why do so many teams fail to achieve goals even after identifying clear targets and strategies? They never meet to review the scoreboards and commit to *do* specific things to reach the targets. Without a consistent cadence of accountability, the team will get lost in the whirlwind—guaranteed! Furthermore, a lack of follow-through on the part of the leader sends a message to the team that the goal is not "wildly important" after all. And that's the real question, isn't it?

Reflection: Lynn Kosinski
Getting Closer

It wasn't our first attempt as a district to restructure the school day in order to maximize time for teachers to meet in collaborative teams. We had been down this road before. But this time it was different. Upon returning from a conference about Professional Learning Communities (PLCs) with Richard DuFour, several staff members, principals, and teachers were energized by the promise of what PLCs could do for student achievement, if done well. *Doing it well* was the key.

So that teachers could meet in PLC groups one afternoon a week, we lengthened school hours the other days. At these meetings, teachers reviewed assessment data and made plans for future instruction based on the data. Most teachers were happy to have this block of time. This weekly cadence gave them a regular opportunity to ponder the data outside the frenzy of the whirlwind.

Still, given their enthusiasm for these meetings, I wondered why I encountered such mixed results when I visited the teams during their collaboration period. While I was there, teams enthusiastically pored over the data. They charted students who exceeded standards and those who needed more time and practice. They talked about successful instructional strategies and opportunities for additional instruction and enrichment for students. However, a few weeks later I would return to the same school and see the same once-highly-engaged teachers floundering in their discussions.

The meetings were losing focus. I heard conversations about the upcoming football game and Aunt Betty's knee replacement. I saw a lineup of teachers at the copy machine, while in another room other teachers had eyes glazed like a dozen doughnuts. What could have possibly gone wrong to move them so off course from the focused conversations they were having just a couple of weeks before?

Obviously, there was a disconnect. Although they had plenty of data to consider and lots of opportunities to share views in these meetings, the team members had no clear agenda, no protocol for accounting for results. They knew how to analyze data, they had lots of ideas for instructional strategies, but they had no real process for following up on these meetings.

We lacked Discipline 4, the "cadence of accountability." Although teachers often discussed their next steps, these commitments were not recorded, scoreboarded, or revisited in a systematic manner in subsequent meetings. Everything was left to chance and individual initiative. Without systematic accounting for their commitments, the team was not really a team.

You can practice Disciplines 1 through 3 with excellence, but until you apply Discipline 4, you aren't progressing—and student learning will suffer.

SECTION 3: Putting It All Together

Now you've learned about each of the 4 Disciplines of Execution. The truth is, each of the disciplines done in isolation will lead to improved results. Turning a fuzzy goal into a WIG by using the From X to Y by When formula will galvanize your team. Tracking your performance on a public scoreboard will immediately engage people. And having a cadence of accountability around any objective always leads to better outcomes. But the Disciplines were not designed to stand alone. They work far better together. They form a system that can solve many of the intractable problems every educator faces. They have been tested and refined by hundreds of organizations and thousands of teams over many years. And if done with fidelity, they work every time.

The 4 Disciplines are simple but applying them is not simplistic. Here in Section 3, we illustrate how these disciplines work together to produce results, show you how to install the system in your organization, and answer some frequently asked questions.

Section 3 contains the following helpful resources:

- Success in the System: The 4 Disciplines of Execution is a proven system for achieving your highest and best goals. You can't pick and choose among the Disciplines—without the total package you will not get the superb results you want.

- A Quick Start Guide for installing the 4 Disciplines of Execution in your organization.

- Frequently Asked Questions

- So Now What?

- Gallery of Scoreboards

Success in the System

What makes the biggest difference between schools that succeed and those that don't?

The education world is abuzz with the movement toward "Collective Teacher Efficacy" (CTE) as the most important factor in student achievement. Collective Teacher Efficacy is more than just teachers making a collective difference. It's the idea that teachers can best improve student outcomes if they work as a team.

In the last few decades, a whole body of CTE research seems to show that teams of teachers working in a cooperative way toward a common goal get better results than individual teachers do when working in isolation. At the same time, research also shows that teams of teachers lack a systematic way to develop CTE; in short, they don't know how to go about becoming teachers who are "collectively efficacious."[15]

That's where the 4 Disciplines of Execution are so powerful. When implemented with fidelity, 4DX is an *operating system* that can help teams achieve their Wildly Important Goals.

You know that your computer won't work without an operating system, like Windows or iOS. The operating system is the software that supports a computer's basic functions, such as executing the various applications on your computer. Without the operating system, your computer wouldn't operate!

4DX is like that. It's an operating system for your school. It's the way you work. And just as you have systems for hiring, professional development, and student interventions, 4DX is your system for achieving your highest priorities, your way of getting important things done.

It all starts with rallying the team around a WIG and the lead measures that support it, all displayed on a compelling scoreboard. The team then reviews the scoreboard each week, asking, "Is the score moving?" "What needs to change?" "What are our commitments for the week?" This systematic process of reviewing and committing and aligning again and again, week after week, brings about Collective Teacher Efficacy!

4DX is a system that literally involves every single member of the school, from the principal to the students, from the teachers to the facilities manager and the bus driver. Everyone is engaged in a winnable game.

The experience of Canyon Ridge High School in Twin Falls, Idaho, demonstrates how 4DX works as a system.

"We were getting disgruntled, hopeless, a little negative about the results we were getting from students," says principal Kasey Teske. "I felt like things were spiraling the wrong way. We had goals, but it was hard to focus on them because nobody really knew what to expect. We believed we had to be flexible about everything because the targets were always changing. We had so many priorities—but which was the most wildly important?"

After studying 4DX, the Canyon Ridge staff set a lofty WIG of increasing the school's graduation rate from 85 percent to 95 percent within four years. They communicated this goal to the students and the parents. "We believed that goal would inspire and drive the cultural changes of better meeting the needs of all students."

Graduation rate is a lag measure, and "it's hard to move the needle on that," says Kasey. "What are you going to monitor to move that lag measure? What's going to be your lead measure? We discussed it and decided that the best thing we could come up with was to monitor passing classes. Each week we would pinpoint the number of students who had passing grades in the courses they were in."

But what mechanism could they adopt to monitor all of that, with hundreds of students and a changing picture every week? Fortunately, the school adopted "early release Mondays," which enabled departments to meet Monday afternoons, compile the data, and report it. Additionally, during that time they could meet students by appointment for accountability conversations with the ones who were not passing. "We had hundreds of conversations with students focused on the goal of passing their courses, and that pushed things in the right direction."

They also adopted some incentives for students who were passing, like a little extra time for lunch. They also held quarterly assemblies to celebrate the increase in passing rates. "It was really high energy." At last, at the end of the final quarter of that academic year, the students sponsored an assembly, and Kasey announced they had reached a 95 percent graduation rate for the first time. "The kids went crazy. You wouldn't think high school students would be excited about something like that, but the energy in that gym was amazing."

Success came to Canyon Ridge because they built a system for achieving WIGs with 4DX as the nucleus.

They began with a paradigm shift about their jobs. They now believed that their job was to "Focus on the Wildly Important Goal" rather than fragmenting their focus over multiple priorities (Discipline 1). They believed that achieving the WIG would positively impact all their other school priorities.

After selecting the WIG as a staff, they selected a lead measure (Discipline 2). They chose the passing rate of all courses as a lead measure, which they saw as predictive of graduation success and readily influenceable and measurable from week to week. The staff reasoned that student success in passing courses at a high rate would greatly impact the graduation rate.

INFLUENCEABLE

Passing Rate – Goal 95%

Our Most Wildly Important Goals

Graduation Rate
Goal 87.3%
Class of 2019

PREDICTIVE

Once the staff set the direction of the goals, they presented the goals to the Student Lead Team for input. The Student Lead Team is made up of five leadership classes, involving about 125 students who represent the student body. The Student Lead Team agreed to the 95 percent WIG and planned how they would share the goals with the entire student body during the Opening Day of School assembly.

In order to act on their lead measure, a few systems and structures within the school were changed. "We had never collected and reviewed data like this before," says Kasey Teske.

Subject	Students Not Passing		△
	Last Week	**This Week**	**Change**
Math	94	109	**15**
ELA	133	131	**-2**
Science	88	101	**13**
Social Studies	137	118	**-19**
Business	40	50	**10**
PE/ Health	13	16	**3**
CTE	43	53	**10**

The principal at Canyon Ridge High School emails the school community weekly with the latest results on progress toward the school WIG of a 95 percent passing rate.

Another systemic change was the early release Monday, which they made up for by longer instruction hours on Tuesdays and Thursdays. As we've seen, this system enabled teachers to meet briefly for WIG Sessions, to review the scoreboard and report on the commitments they make. Then, each week, Principal Teske would email a report to the entire school community. Here is an actual sample:

Hello to the River Hawks of Canyon Ridge High School! As promised, I'm reporting this week's progress on our Wildly Important Goal to graduate 95% of our students.

To achieve that goal, we track every week the number of students who are passing their classes. **This week we gained 53 failing grades in semester 1. But I'm sure we'll turn that around next week!**

A big public scoreboard tracks progress toward the WIG in the main hallway at Canyon Ridge.

The lever chart illustrates the WIG itself, along with the lag measure. The chart (seen below) tracks graduation rate over several years. The chart on the left compares progress toward the lag measure over several past quarters.

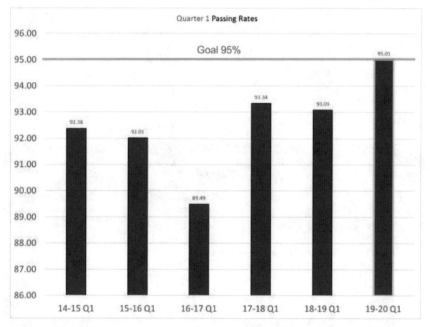

Each quarter, Canyon Ridge reports progress toward a 95% graduation rate by comparing the number of passing students with previous quarters.

The Canyon Ridge system also calls for students to have personal WIGs as well. During advisory periods, students check their grades, calculate their GPA, and graph it. Any student with a D or F grade meets one-on-one with a teacher for additional support. Here is an example of a student's personal scoreboard:

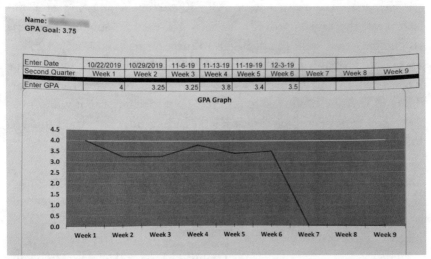

Name:									
GPA Goal: 3.75									

Enter Date	10/22/2019	10/29/2019	11-6-19	11-13-19	11-19-19	12-3-19			
Second Quarter	Week 1	Week 2	Week 3	Week 4	Week 5	Week 6	Week 7	Week 8	Week 9
Enter GPA	4	3.25	3.25	3.8	3.4	3.5			

This student has set her own WIG to graduate with a 3.75 GPA. She tracks her GPA—her lag measure—every week.

The results? As we have seen, from the first semester of focusing on the WIG and lead measures, the school saw an unprecedented 95 percent passing rate! Without a 4DX system across the school community, they probably would not have achieved this goal.

Now that the 4DX system is in place, everyone thinks differently at Canyon Ridge High School. The paradigm of what can be achieved has changed. A great example of that is what happened in the pandemic year of 2020–2021, according to Kasey Teske:

When we started to hold school online half the time, our passing rate plunged because students weren't doing their assignments online. It was a huge problem. They were unused to working online—too many distractions, too unfamiliar. So I thought, "How can we move this measure? We've got to do something to fix this." I felt passionate about this. It was a big, obvious lead measure that had to move. Nobody had any solutions.

So we said, "Let's focus. Let's get the kids to start off the week right. We'll just target Monday's online assignments, make them simple and meaningful, and measure the completion of Monday assignments." The idea was to have every student complete an assignment every Monday in every class and track it.

The first week started with a 30–40 percent submission rate, but each week the rate improved. Students got used to submitting online assignments, and soon things began to turn around and normalize. Kasey says he probably would not have figured out what to do without the 4DX system of unrelenting focus, data gathering, and intensive accountability. "Anytime you measure progress on a specific goal, it will probably improve; but once you decide it's the most wildly important thing to do, it makes a huge difference to your way of thinking."

How 4DX Works as a System for Closing Performance Gaps. Many schools like Canyon Ridge now use 4DX as an operating system for accomplishing their goals. Adopting 4DX usually involves a few changes to entrenched systems and processes, but the rewards definitely exceed the cost of doing so.

The 4DX system at Hiller Elementary, Madison Heights, Michigan, illustrates those rewards.

In a spirit of true collaboration, focus, and an unwavering belief in the potential of *all* students, the staff at Hiller Elementary became nationally recognized by the National Association of ESEA State Program Administrators for their efforts serving English Language Learners (ELL). In a school where 75 percent of the students are not native English speakers, and of these, 63 percent are refugees displaced from their home countries, you can imagine the challenges facing the teaching staff.

Student goal setting was cited by Hiller Principal Brad Sassack as one of the underpinnings to their success and ultimately their national distinction. Not only were staff members laser focused on their highest priority—closing student proficiency gaps—students also shared this focus. Students maintained Leadership Notebooks with a special section for their WIGs. Every student routinely tracked progress toward individualized WIGs.

English as a Second Language (ESL) teacher Shaima Shammas systematically tracked the progress of the ELL students she taught in a small

group for an hour a day four days a week. Each student recorded progress on individualized WIGs in their notebooks after each assessment
cycle and celebrated their growth. Shaima's unique contribution was in
the development of lead measures. Outwardly, it appeared as if all the
students had the same lead measures, i.e., read every night and complete
a reading homework sheet; however, the measures were tailored to each
student. They chose their own readings and worksheets focused on a
specific skill, strategy, or concept. A student reading a non-fiction book
might work on identifying text features or summarizing, while other students worked on different skill sets.

The next day, the student would put a star on the scoreboard if they
completed their lead measures for the previous day. Then they reviewed
their progress on the lead measures. Shaima also conferred with the students one-on-one each week.

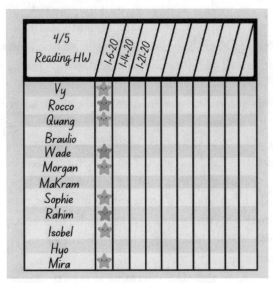

**Example of class scoreboard at Hiller Elementary tracking individual work on
lead measures.**

Results of this systematic approach have been impressive. On the annual State of Michigan standardized assessment (M-STEP) English Language Arts test, English Learners grew their proficiency rate by 10 percent. On the World-Class Instructional Design and Assessment (WIDA)
to measure students' language proficiency, 91.5 percent of Limited En-

glish Proficient (LEP) learners showed growth from the previous year.

Brad Sassack recalls meeting then fourth grade student Ghalia during his first year as principal. She was "a student that we could count on. One of our leaders. She was a go-getter among her group." But that had not always been the case. Ghalia came from Iraq, arriving at Hiller Elementary as a non-English-speaking (NES) second grader. According to Reading Specialist Lindsay Staskowski, "Ghalia did not know English at all. And when she was learning the language, she was very afraid to make a mistake. So, she was quiet and shy and didn't like to talk." She was "hesitant" and "nervous." "She never ate at school because was so nervous—new school, new country, new language."

Two years later, when listening to the daily morning announcements broadcast over the PA system, Ghalia's second grade teacher was shocked to hear Ghalia, now in the fourth grade, sharing the morning news in a poised, confident voice. Ghalia's public speaking didn't stop there. As a fifth grade student, Ghalia confidently made a presentation during a "Leadership Night" to the entire audience of parents, community members, and Board of Education representatives. Upon exiting Hiller Elementary, Ghalia no longer needed ESL services. To a great extent, Ghalia succeeded because of the focused goals, targeted commitments, and accountability system brought to Hiller by 4DX.

The Hiller school community believes in the genius of all students and celebrates their cultures. This was supported through project-based lead measures such as hosting diversity nights which included sharing foods from student homelands. One year a large number of families gained US citizenship. To highlight this accomplishment, a big celebration was held at the school where the mayor came and honored the families.

Another reward of the 4DX operating system is the creation of lifelong goal setters. A third grade student in Colorado Springs, Colorado, demonstrated she is building that life skill. She had not only an academic WIG but also a personal WIG, which was to keep her bedroom clean. To scoreboard her WIG, she created a rubric that defined levels of cleanliness. Each day after school, she scanned her room and gave it a rating based on the rubric. She then noted the rating on her personal scoreboard, which showed a continuous trend of improved room cleanliness. When asked who helped her create the scoreboard and rubric, she responded that she created them by herself, using the knowledge she had obtained from using 4DX to track her academic WIG. Proactivity and a transfer of knowledge led to a successful personal achievement (not to mention the likelihood of happy parents)! Think about the power of our students transferring the 4DX system to their own life goals!

How to Do 4DX Online. When the global pandemic of 2020 hit, brick and mortar schools across the world were forced to close, some for over a year. To keep educating children, teachers were required to pivot and embrace online learning—for many of them, a new and untried instructional method.

Before the pandemic, Michelle had a WIG accountability system that ran like a well-oiled machine. In her second grade classroom in New York City, students met regularly to check in with their Accountability Partners and encourage them to do their best. In the blink of an eye, all of that changed. Michelle suddenly found herself teaching a classroom of second graders via Zoom. Michelle knew how effective 4DX could be, especially the student-to-student Accountability Partners. She was not willing to abandon the idea just because she was teaching online. Instead, she embraced the challenge.

It would have been easy to throw up her hands and toss student WIGs aside until things got back to normal. However, no one knew when that would be. Knowing the power of 4DX, Michelle got to work creating an online system for scoreboarding and Accountability Partner meetings.

This is what the 4 Disciplines looked like in Michelle's classroom.

Discipline 1: Focus on the Wildly Important:

Our class will move up 69 reading levels by June. To meet this goal, each student will grow three levels over the academic year.

Discipline 2: Act on the Lead Measures

- Read daily for at least 30 minutes independently.
- Apply reading strategy daily during independent reading.

Discipline 3: Keep a Compelling Scoreboard

- Each student tracks his/her lead measures on a reading log using a graph and supporting documents.
- A digital classroom scoreboard is updated and visible.

Michelle transformed her beautiful classroom bulletin board into a fun and engaging electronic scoreboard with a solar system theme. As the scoreboard was updated, a rocket ship and astronaut floated from planet to planet, representing advances in reading growth. The students loved it! They looked forward to logging in to see how far the astronaut moved each day based on their reading efforts.

This engaging online scoreboard used a rocket and an astronaut to track student progress toward a reading WIG.

Discipline 4: Create a Cadence of Accountability

To keep a cadence of accountability going among students, Michelle established Reading Goal Clubs. Every Friday students go into online breakout rooms with their Reading Goal Club, and each student has an assigned role in fostering a useful conversation. These are the roles:

- A Student Facilitator supports his classmates, making sure they are focused on the learning task.

- A Recorder records how many reading levels they have moved up as a group.

- A Timekeeper keeps track of time, announcing when they reach half time and when time is nearly up.

- A Student Leader Reporter returns to the main room and reports to the whole class the club's progress toward meeting their goal.

Before moving to breakout rooms, Michelle reminds students of the work they are to do. In the breakout room, students discuss and analyze their reading goals. You would hear these questions asked:

- Let's look at your progress graph. How do you feel when looking at the progress you made?

- What steps can you take moving forward to keep moving up your reading level?

- Do you feel proud of your progress?

- Do you notice the difference between how you were reading before and how you are reading now?

- What do you think were the steps that helped you accomplish this goal?

- Have you learned new strategies that you can use to move up to the next level?

After the breakout session, the class scoreboard is updated, and the astronaut moves forward in the virtual solar system.

Michelle shares the following tips based on her experience. "Make sure you keep the cadence of accountability consistent. Teach the students how to fill out the graph and save it digitally on their computer or tablet. Also, teach them how to converse in their goal clubs and how to perform their leadership roles before launching. Provide students with sentence starters to facilitate the flow of the conversation."

As Michelle's experience demonstrates, with great determination and commitment, 4DX can be incorporated in both face-to-face and on-line settings.

How the 4DX System Works With Very Young Students. It's never too early to install the 4DX system in the lives of students. At Hyledar Vanke City Kindergarten in Qindao, China, they adopted English fluency as a WIG with the lag measure of speaking English 1,000 times in 14 days across the school. The problem was that 80 of the students were only three years old! How do you explain this lofty goal to them?

School coach Paul Chen Junhao solved the problem by turning the WIG into a game. The little ones were told that if they spoke English once a day, they would cross a yellow line on a scoreboard. If they all crossed the line, they would have a big celebration. The scoreboard was prominently displayed at the building entrance.

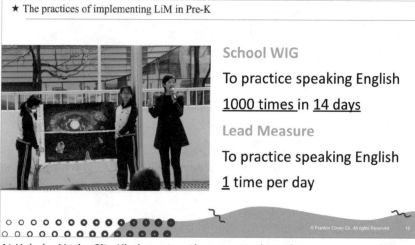

At Hyledar Vanke City Kindergarten, they constantly update progress on their WIG and lead measure.

Parents sent to the school, photos of their kindergarten children practicing English.

Students practiced English with their parents each night at home. Then they would color in a square in their personal leadership notebooks and add a sticker to a classroom scoreboard. Parents were highly supportive, even sending photos to teachers of their children practicing their English.

Instead of 1,000 practice sessions, the students held 1,712 sessions over a two-week period. The results of acting on this lead measure were impressive! On a common assessment administered monthly, Hyledar Vanke City Kindergarten saw a dramatic increase in English scores.

THEY MADE IT!

In total, it was 1712 times at last, which is 170% up to the standard WIG of 1000 times.

The kindergarten students exceeded the goal of 1,000 English practice sessions by 712 practices.

As the students at Hyledar kindergarten showed, once you put laser focus on the single thing that has to get done and you get everyone systematically aligned and engaged behind it, there is nothing that you can't accomplish—even with the youngest of learners.

How 4DX Works as a Schoolwide Operating System. Installing an operating system like 4DX in a school is not a small thing. It requires investment in training, collaboration, and creation of new tools. It also requires a certain change in thinking. Unsurprisingly, many educators hesitate to commit themselves and their schools to such an all-encompassing change.

Craig Gunter is the former principal of Carmel Elementary in Hesperia, California. He's an educational scholar, a voracious consumer of educational research on a continuous quest to bring the very best practices to his work. When he encountered the 4DX system, he was already well versed in goal setting, writing SMART goals, and creating Strategic Improvement Plans. However, something struck Craig as different about 4DX—was this a way to actually execute his goals? Was it something much more than setting a goal or writing a huge Strategic Improvement Plan burdened with too many strategies to manage?

Craig was curious, but he needed to prove to himself that 4DX worked before committing his school to such an overhaul. For one thing, he was principal of a school serving the students in one of the poorest cities in one of the poorest counties in the state. The school had an enrollment of over 700 students of which close to 90 percent were economically disadvantaged—and the poverty trend was rising. A trend that was *not* rising was state standardized assessment performance. So, Craig was not about to ask his staff or his students to try yet another new strategy unless he was completely convinced the strategy would work.

He decided to try the system on himself. He had been thinking about adding running to his fitness program. What better way to put 4DX to the test than to set a Wildly Important Goal around running? He set a WIG with the lag measure of running not at all to running a 5K by February 25 (Discipline 1). His lead measures would be running three times a week and eating healthy meals (Discipline 2). He kept a scoreboard on a calendar on which he daily tracked his lead measures (Discipline 3). Finally, Craig's wife Kristie met with him to review progress and make new commitments (Discipline 4).

He also included his school in the new goal. He told everybody in the school what he was doing, and staff and students all became excited as they tracked their principal's progress toward his goal. After months of training and involving all his students in his WIG and his progress, the big day arrived. Through focus and fidelity to the 4DX process, Craig ran a 5K on February 25, achieving his Wildly Important Goal. The whole student body celebrated.

With this personal victory under his belt, Craig was ready to roll out the full 4DX process to his school.

What about students who are reluctant to accept 4DX? Once students get adjusted to the 4DX system, they find it quite motivating. For example, Tim Vandenberg, a 25-year veteran classroom teacher at Carmel Elementary and an adjunct professor in the School of Education at the University of Redlands, found he could energize a class full of discouraged sixth graders by getting them focused on a WIG.

Tim privately shared each student's previous state assessment score with them. This became the X for their Wildly Important Goal. Next, they discussed their individual target (Y) for the assessment in May

(When). Lead measures came in the form of extra lessons students were to complete to a certain level of mastery. Students tracked their progress toward lesson completion on individual trackers. Tim further leveraged the power of keeping score to boost the motivation of his students. Each week he totaled the amount of time each student spent on the computer-based assignments. The top ten students were celebrated each week and earned "class cash" to spend on things like "select your own seat for a day." A strong cadence of accountability system ensured students worked toward their WIG with a high level of commitment.

What was the outcome of Tim Vandenberg's efforts? A 34 percent boost in scores compared to a two percent growth by their grade level district peers! The same group of students that had a 14 percent passing rate as fifth grade students now boasted a 48 percent passing rate in the sixth grade. This kind of outcome seems unlikely at first glance, but once you understand the principle-based methodology of the 4 Disciplines, it is totally doable and predictable. The key is in the integrated system of the 4 Disciplines. All four disciplines are needed. Bypass or neglect any one of them and the system collapses.

How 4DX Works With an MTSS Framework. Multi-Tier System of Supports (MTSS) is a framework for providing customized support to students. The idea is to ascertain a student's level of academic progress and then create supporting mechanisms specifically designed to help that student. The whole child is the focus of MTSS, targeting social/emotional development as well as academic growth.

School districts across the United States have adopted the MTSS framework to comprehensively meet students' needs. Can an MTSS process benefit from 4DX? How does 4DX support MTSS? Northville Public Schools answers that question.

"If not here, then where?"—a common question asked by the Superintendent of Northville Public Schools, Mary Kay Gallagher. As a leader with great vision who takes the advancement of a tradition of excellence in the high-performing school district very seriously, Mary Kay makes sure that district goals are tightly aligned vertically and horizontally to ensure all students attain core competencies. While she and her staff could easily rest on their laurels as one of the top-ranked school districts in the State of Michigan, instead they continuously challenge themselves to deliver stronger results every day on behalf of every child they serve.

Northville's long-standing history of early intervention, which has grown into the current MTSS framework, keeps the rate of special education students well below the state average. In 2019–20, the Michigan's special-education identification rate was 13.4 percent, while at Northville it was 5.9 percent.

As we saw in our discussion of Discipline 1: Focus on the Wildly Important, WIGs in Northville cascade in tight alignment from the district down to the student level. For example, here is the district literacy WIG:

"All students will demonstrate growth in literacy skills by June 20XX, as indicated below."

a. All kindergarten through seventh grade students will demonstrate growth in literacy as measured by NWEA (target=at least 60% achieving NWEA projected growth) and proficiency on M-STEP and local assessments.

b. 100% of kindergarten students will be proficient on the state assessment in reading, consistent with the provisions of MCL 380.1280f (the state third grade reading requirement).

c. At least 92% of students in grades eight through eleven will demonstrate growth in literacy as measured by college- and career-readiness benchmarks in Evidence Based Reading and Writing in English Language Arts on PSAT 8/9, PSAT 10 and SAT, and local assessments.

This straightforward job to be done and systematic MTSS process sets the stage for teachers to get to work with a clear end in mind.

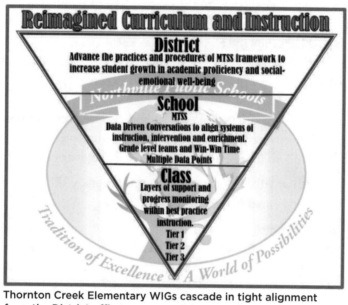

Thornton Creek Elementary WIGs cascade in tight alignment from the District office.

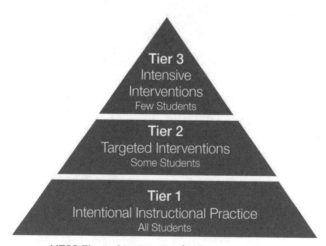

MTSS Tiers of Instruction/Intervention

Every school's primary goal is to ensure all teachers provide high-quality instruction to all students (Tier 1). About 80 percent of students are expected to meet learning targets in this tier. Approximately 10–15 percent of students might require more focused and supplemental instruction (Tier 2), and 1–5 percent of students might need more comprehensive programming (Tier 3).

To gauge student progress in reading, Northville District has a comprehensive assessment plan, and each assessment within the plan has a specific purpose. A nationally normed assessment is administered at the beginning of the school year to determine baseline knowledge and skills of students. At designated intervals, this same assessment is administered to gauge progress toward specific goals. A benchmark assessment tool is also administered periodically, to identify student growth in instruction and independent reading levels. Teachers also administer informal assessments of their own. The state summative assessment is administered at the end of the year. 4DX is designed to take advantage of this rich store of data.

The MTSS and 4DX goal setting process is uniform in all elementary schools across the district. Each building-based MTSS team maintains a weekly cadence of WIG meetings. The team (comprising a learning consultant, resource room teachers, speech and language teachers, psychologist, social worker, classroom teacher, and principal) meets to discuss students who need targeted academic or behavioral support. They review assessment data, update scoreboards, and make commitments to support the students.

Progress Monitoring

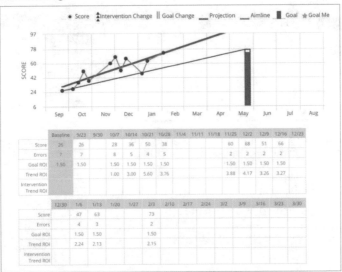

The Thornton Creek Elementary scoreboard shows the trend line to meet the WIG as well as the actual performance trend line. As you can see, they are well ahead of where they hoped to be!

Thornton Creek Grade Level MTTS planning

Grade Level:　First Grade　　　Date:　10/7/2020

Who: Students	What: Concerns	Action Steps Accommodations teacher has taken to address concerns	Action Steps for Team Commitments Additional Data Needed
▮	Writing and math support	Prompting - prompt dependent	Collect data to determine where she is with writing and math skills On task Off task *Review accommodation log data Develop checklist for task completion and reward system(support will be given to help implement the system) Timeline - will be discussed at 10/14 meeting 10/22 Observations were conducted, visuals are being made and push in support Mondays and Tuesdays at 11:00
▮	Monitor at this point - higher than group Attention concerns		Continue - check in check out Return to TIER I - Monitor academic progress
▮	27%ile 32%ile		Collect more data - reading a to z Pull ▮ into reading group *she was flagged to start in spring - never attended zoom in spring Monitor - ▮ 10/22 ▮ joined group 10/13. Set PM goal

This is a record of commitments the team at Thornton Creek Elementary made one week to provide targeted support to students.

To assist teachers in identifying lead measures, the district provides a brainstormed list of strategies they might use. The lists are categorized by tier.

Reading WIG
Wildly Important Goal

NWEA _____

Foundational Skills
Language and Writing
Literature and Informational
Vocabulary Use and Functions

F&P _____

Thinking Within Text
Thinking Beyond Text
Thinking About Text
Fluency

Reading goal:

_____ will go from an instruction level _____ to an instruction level _____ by _____.

Classroom Strategic Plan of Action/Lead Measures:

Tier 2	C	WW		Teacher Notes:
Strategic, Small Group, Needs-Based Learning 1:3-1:5	☐	☐	Targeted Guided Reading or Small Group Instruction (3-4 days)	
	☐	☐	Systematic Phonological awareness intervention	
	☐	☐	Phonemic awareness with visuals	
	☐	☐	Visual Cues and concrete examples	
	☐	☐	Scaffold responses - Graphic organizers for responding to reading	
	☐	☐	Monitoring comprehension scaffolds (stop and jot, sticky notes, etc.)	
	☐	☐	Sight word/vocabulary interventions	
	☐	☐	Academic leader support	
	☐	☐	Provide frequent, immediate, positive feedback	
	☐	☐	At home reading and skill practice	
	☐	☐	MTSS Intervention Support	
	☐	☐		
	☐	☐		
Tier 3 Intensive Strategic Needs-Based Learning	☐	☐	Targeted Guided Reading or Small Group Instruction (5 days)	
	☐	☐	Academic leader support	
	☐	☐	At home reading and skill practice	
	☐	☐	MTSS Intervention Support	

Thornton Creek Elementary WIG and candidate strategies for lead measures appropriate to each tier.

Grade level teams meet weekly to gauge progress on their "Behind-the-Scenes Proficiency WIGs." The teachers themselves write these WIGs to identify what they will do to help students reach reading-proficiency targets. Teachers record progress toward their lag measure at the baseline, second, and third testing intervals. They also determine lead measures, track them, discuss their impact, and adjust as needed.

Academic Team
Reading WIG Data
Behind the Scenes Proficiency WIG

Classroom:

_____ class will improve from _____% to _____% of students reading at or above proficiency as measured by Fountas and Pinnell Benchmark Assessment by June 2021 (spring testing).

Second Testing Interval	Final Testing Interval

Lead Measures
- Complete three progress monitoring cycles.
- Triangulation of three data sources three times a year
- Create specialized intervention/enrichment plans for 100% of our students three times a year.

Teacher WIG and lead measures (private) from Thornton Creek Elementary School.

Students set their own individual WIGs based on the classroom WIG. They use a key tool with strategies indicating how to think within, beyond, and about the text. This tool enables the students to reflect on their reading progress within their specific tier and to make commitments to improve their progress.

As teachers privately scoreboard progress toward proficiency WIGs, students track their progress in individual leadership portfolios. Like teachers, they too have an ongoing cadence of accountability with a peer. Additionally, both schoolwide and classroom growth scoreboards are posted publicly to show the students if they are winning and to help motivate them toward reaching their collective goal.

This schoolwide scoreboard shows how each classroom at each grade level is progressing toward the school WIG.

Northville district teachers are totally committed to helping students reach their potential. And students themselves round out this robust system of goal setting, analysis, and monitoring, by setting their own WIGs. Catherine Gibson, a learning consultant in the district, describes the system this way:

"Our (student) Reading WIG documents incorporate the Strategic Wheel of Action (Fountas and Pinnell) to help students choose a goal focus and share lead measures or steps they will take to help them improve in reading. This goal setting process develops into a gradual release over time and provides for differentiated lead measures within goal setting. In addition, a weekly reflection allows students the opportunity to evaluate their practice toward the goal and how it has helped them as a reader. The reflection component creates intrinsic motivation, an understanding of learning and an ownership of the student's own learning path."

Clearly, 4DX is ideal for helping schools within the MTSS framework to achieve targeted goals at each tier.

How the 4DX System Impacts Individual Students. It's the impact of the 4DX system on the heart and mind of the individual student that really matters. The story of one little girl bears out just how much the little victories won by children guided through the Disciplines can mean to them.

A substitute teacher named Rose often replaced one kindergarten teacher who was gone a lot. Rose found the class chaotic because of the lack of continuity, and she dreaded being called in to sub. All the students were challenging, but one little girl named Mikayla stood out—she was a wanderer. She would slide out the door and disappear, leaving Rose exasperated and searching the building for her. Mikayla was both socially and academically adrift.

Rose encountered Mikayla again in the next few years. One day the little girl came home from the library to find that her mother had passed away. Completely traumatized, she refused to go back to school, and when she finally did, she acted out and had trouble calming down. Meanwhile, Rose developed a relationship with Mikayla's father and soon they were married—Rose was now Mikayla's new mom and a true advocate for the emotionally distraught girl.

The challenges never went away. Mikayla cried, fought, and frustrated her parents. It was heartbreaking for both of them to watch Mikayla make so little progress. When the school suggested she be retained, Rose decided to enroll her in Carmel Elementary. Rose knew the reputation of Carmel as a "Leadership School" and was well acquainted with Tim Vandenberg.

Still academically behind and still carrying a chip on her shoulder, Mikayla entered sixth grade at Carmel Elementary in Mr. Vandenberg's classroom. "He's so nerdy," Mikayla would say. "He makes dumb jokes." But over time, her criticisms of Mr. Vandenberg gradually shifted. Her attitude toward school slowly evolved as well. In the highly engaging classroom, under the leadership of a teacher who never gives up on children and who ensures that all students account for their goals, Mikayla eventually became highly motivated. She worked tirelessly all year to achieve her WIG. When the State Assessment results came in, Mikayla passed—above grade level!

Excited by this victory, with a new belief in herself, Mikayla headed to middle school. When she picked up her seventh grade schedule, she asked Rose, "What are all these H's next to the classes on my schedule?" "Honors," her mother responded. "You placed into honors classes." Stunned but ever so proud, Mikayla couldn't wait to return to Carmel Elementary to share the great news with Mr. Vandenberg.

By adopting the 4DX system, schools create a culture where students like Mikayla can thrive. The remarkable story of Carmel Elementary bears this out. That first year after Principal Gunter put the system in place, a reading-proficiency WIG was set, lead measures selected, and scoreboards posted to show progress. Acting on common lead measures—reading 30 minutes per night and completing accelerated worksheets—the school managed to score 85 percent on the state comprehension assessment. Where the previous year only 240 students met their Accelerated Reader accuracy goal, the next year more than 600 students met it. The one-year growth was so dramatic that a representative from Renaissance Learning, Inc., the developer of Accelerated Reader, called Principal Gunter to ask what they were doing at Carmel Elementary to achieve such success.

Now that we have shared the 4DX system with myriad schools, we have many success stories like these. They are not surprising. After all, hundreds of companies, including the hotel company Marriott Worldwide, use 4DX systematically to reach their desired results. Now, individual students, teachers, schools, and districts know how to do the same with a focus on a few Wildly Important Goals, coupled with high-leverage activities (lead measures), a scoreboard, and Accountability Partners.

Throughout this book we have highlighted many success stories, shared tips for success, and traps to avoid. Many educational leaders can now do the same. For example, Trevor Dietrich, a principal in California and long-time proponent of 4DX, adds the following insights based on his years of experience:

"I made some errors in my initial WIG. I had about five lead measures, which were too many."

"Fake it 'til you make it. It doesn't matter if you believe 4DX will work or not, it works. You just sometimes have to jump in and do it and then you become a believer as you see it."

"Be careful of setting lag measures based on the class average. The problem with that is that the high-performing kids are pulling the average up and your low performers are pulling it down . . . and they all recognize that."

"The idea of differentiating goals is important. Since schools work with standardized tests, teachers often want to set standardized goals— *First graders should be reading at a running record level of 16 by the end of the year*. But that's baloney. Some should be reading at a level 24 by the end of the year, and some are going to work really, really hard to get to a level 8."

"For administrators, make it as easy as possible for teachers to jump in. Create templates. Remove obstacles so teachers can do the best work they can do. Put structures in place so 4DX can happen."

The fact is: the principles of focus, leverage, engagement, and accountability as contained in 4DX are incredibly powerful when applied to whole organizations of any kind, be it a school or an enterprise. In education, 4DX is a superb tool for developing collective teacher efficacy. When the Disciplines are systematically applied, positive results are virtually guaranteed.

A Quick Start Guide to 4DX Implementation

The following guide will help you "quick start" the 4DX system within your organization. You will find steps to follow based on your function:

- District Superintendent/Cabinet Level
- Principal Level
- Teacher Level
- Student Level

Don't forget to celebrate progress at each level!

DISTRICT SUPERINTENDENT/CABINET LEVEL

STEP	ACTION
1	Narrow the focus of the District Improvement Plan to one or two Widly Important Goals.
2	Determine your lag measure data source.
3	Write your WIG in a From X to Y by When format.
4	Involve every cabinet leader in creating a WIG for their department.
5	Encourage cabinet leaders to meet with their respective department personnel to determine lead measures.
6	Create a scoreboarding system, involve cabinet leaders in this process.
7	Establish a regular and ongoing cadence of accountability.

TIPS

Lead by modeling—Stay engaged in the process, but don't micromanage.

Clear the path—Be of service to cabinet leaders and help remove barriers to success.

Remain curious and visible—Visit department personnel, not just the leader. Ask how they're doing and if there is anything you can do to assist.

Celebrate progress—A personal note or email to the leader or team can be a big deposit and may keep the team motivated.

WATCH OUT

Stay focused. There will always be competing priorities demanding your attention.

4DX must become your operating system, not an add on or "flavor of the month."

PRINCIPAL LEVEL

STEP	ACTION (FOR ACADEMIC WIG)	
1	Conduct a 4DX book study or overview.	
2	Narrow the focus of your strategic improvement plan to one Wildly Important Goal aligned to the priorities of your district.	
3	Determine your lag (summative) measure data source.	
4	Determine diagnostic and interim assessments and administration timelines.	
	GROWTH WIG	*PROFICIENCY WIG*
5	Write your **public** WIG in a From X to Y by When format, focused on the **growth**.	Write your **private** WIG in a From X to Y by When format, focused on the **proficiency**.
6	Provide time for teachers to create "pick lists" of possible lead measures for students.	Provide time for teachers to review data and generate their lead measures.
7	Create classroom scoreboards.	Create staff WIG templates/trackers.
8	Determine a common cadence of accountability time for the whole school or grade.	Determine a common cadence of accountability time for teacher teams. Schedule these meetings on the master calendar.
9	Celebrate progress during morning announcements, schoolwide assemblies, virtual meetings, etc.	Celebrate success—notes, shout outs, etc.

TIPS

Formative assessments are important as they allow teachers to adjust instruction and influence lead measures.

If possible, create a private, staff only synergy room where teams can hold their cadence of accountability meetings and private data can be posted.

Success is in the systems; they should not be an afterthought.

WATCH OUT

Allowing each classroom or teacher to create their own scoreboard is encouraged. However, when first learning the 4DX process we recommend using common scoreboard templates to ensure appropriate data is represented.

Commit or crumble. If you do not maintain a strong cadence of accountability to discuss both student and staff progress, the system will crumble.

TEACHER LEVEL

STEP	ACTION (FOR ACADEMIC WIG)
1	Post your classroom WIG and scoreboard in a visible and accessible location.
2	Create a standard WIG plan template for student use.
3	Determine systems for success. Consider when the classroom scoreboard will be updated and who will lead the conversation.
4	Involve students in brainstorming celebrations for milestones achieved.
5	Teach students how to hold a cadence of accountability conversation.

TIPS

When first integrating the 4DX process in your classroom, it could be helpful to have common student lead measures. After you have established strong 4DX systems and routines in your classroom, you can then consider differentiating lead measures by students or groups of students.

Remember, this is a new process for you and your students. Don't expect perfection and don't give up! Stay the course.

WATCH OUT

It is easy to become consumed by the whirlwind.

STUDENT LEVEL

STEP	ACTION
1	Hold a classroom discussion about the purpose of goal setting.
2	Create a thoughtful lesson plan to introduce 4DX.
3	Model the completion of student WIG plans, step-by-step.
4	Establish student-to-student Accountability Partners and determine when they will meet each week.

TIPS

Make it fun! Teach students special cheers or hand signals to encourage their Accountability Partner.

WATCH OUT

Don't expect students to automatically remember when to update their scoreboards and trackers. They will need to be reminded until this becomes a habit.

Frequently Asked Questions

How many WIGs should teachers have?

Remember the principle of focus: the more WIGs you have, the less likely you are to achieve them with excellence. So, you should have no more than two to three WIGs. When you are first learning the 4 Disciplines, you should start with just one WIG.

Our district wants us to adopt a WIG to improve proficiency. What kind of scoreboard should we use?

Proficiency scoreboards track changes in lag measures by percentage, as in the example below. Caution: Scoreboards tracking individual student progress should be kept in a private location.

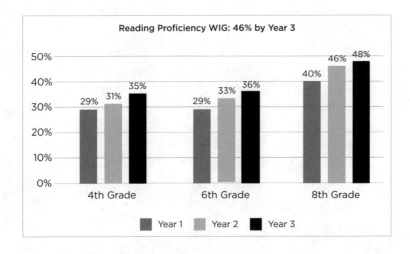

How can we create scoreboards that don't embarrass people?

No public scoreboard should ever embarrass an individual student, teacher, or group. Obviously, scoreboards track achievements, and some people achieve more than others. The best lag measure for a public scoreboard is a universal growth measure: "All students will show growth from their own baseline number." There is no need to show how much growth individuals achieve; you can simply aggregate the growth numbers to show that everyone is progressing. This kind of scoreboard is motivating for children as well as the community. It shows that teachers believe all students can grow. Additionally, many teacher evaluation systems are tied to student growth.

What is a good schoolwide WIG?

An effective schoolwide WIG closes the most critical gap for your team. It is the one thing that is so important nothing else matters very much by comparison. It is also easily understood and easily tracked.

Does a WIG always have to be academic?

No. The WIG closes a critical gap, which might be academic, behavioral, structural, or even financial. For example, you might have a widespread problem with classroom discipline as indicated by a high rate of suspensions. Reducing suspensions might become your lag measure.

What if staff members resist adopting or participating in the 4 Disciplines?

Try to determine the root cause of their resistance. Ask yourself, is this a pattern of behavior they often exhibit when something is new? Do they need to see it work before making a commitment to a process or program? Are they confused? Do they understand what is being asked of them? Ask a lot of questions. Be clear about your intentions. Offer support. Be patient. When they start seeing results, resistant staffers will likely fall in line with the others.

How do we know if we have the right lead measures?

Before choosing lead measures, teams engage in reflective conversations, analysis of available data, and scrutiny of their professional practice. Usually, educators know the right thing to do. What is more often needed is fidelity to the process and time to see results. Ask yourself these questions:

- Is the lead measure moving the lag measure? If so, be careful about abandoning too soon something that is working.

- Is the lag measure moving enough? If not, you might consider raising the standard of performance on the lead measure. Remember, the lever has to move a lot for the rock to move a little.

- Is the team keeping accurate score of the lead measures? If not, the team may have misconceptions about the effectiveness of the lead measure.

- How long has the team been working at the lead measure? In our experience, it takes multiple weeks for a team to form a habit. We encourage you to stay the course and not get bored or restless with your carefully selected lead measures.

If the lead measure is making no difference after a thorough trial, consider replacing it.

What if the lead measure is moving but not the lag measure?

There are a few possible explanations for this:

- First, are you able to monitor the lag measure? If you don't do predictive assessments, such as formative or local common assessments, you might not be able to tell what's happening with the lag measure.

- Have you allowed enough time for the lead measure to affect the lag measure? Moving the lag measure takes time. Be patient and follow the process faithfully.

- Do you need to adjust the lead measure? Consider this possibility last. After all, if you analyzed your data and chose your lead measure carefully, you should be on the right path. If not, you need to find a replacement lead measure that will influence the lag.

How can I ensure the success of the 4 Disciplines in my school?

The key to success is thoughtful planning of these things:

- Ownership
- Timeline
- Tools
- Expectations

Involve all stakeholders in creating the WIGs and lead measures. Collaborate on creating scoreboards. Get consensus on times and places for WIG Sessions. Involvement leads to commitment!

Create a timeline that ensures all stakeholders know exactly when the data analysis is to be completed, WIGs established, lead measures determined, scoreboards created, and cadence meetings calendared.

Create or acquire common tools such as data tracking spreadsheets, lead measure trackers, and scoreboards. Don't let the process stall because participants don't have access to the right tools, most of which the team can create centrally.

Finally, be clear about expectations. People are busy and can easily forget to follow through, especially when a process is new. Make sure training takes place. Send reminders of key events and model adherence to the timeline and initiative.

How many WIGs should individual students have?

A student with one WIG is more likely to achieve it with excellence than a student with many WIGs. When first learning the process, students should set one WIG and focus on it. After they understand the process, they might set both a personal WIG and an academic WIG.

What is the best way to help students choose lead measures? Should students or teachers select lead measures?

Start with two lead measures common to all students for a specific WIG. Once teachers and students establish the routines of recording and reporting on the lead measures, you can guide students to choose their own measures. To this end, create pick lists of strategies/lead measures based on skill gap areas such as fluency, comprehension, decoding, etc.

Students can then choose two lead measures from the appropriate list. More sophisticated students might even create their own lead measures.

Do students need to track lead measures daily?

No. Students might track lead measures daily, but others might be recorded one, two, or three times per week, depending on the focus of the lead measure or need of the student.

Are five- and six-year-old students too young to understand this process?

Not at all! Young students understand goals such as *Learn to tie your shoe by October* or *Learn all the letters on this alphabet page by January.*

How do you track lead measures with very young students?

We have seen great ideas in classrooms around the world. Consider having students record each activity by coloring a box or putting a sticker on their scoreboard.

What if students don't do their lead measures?

You'll want to get to the root cause of this. Do students understand what is being asked of them? Is the lead measure appropriate—too hard or too easy? Do you routinely talk about and celebrate lead measures in class? Are you asking students to complete lead measures outside of school hours and if so, do they have the proper support at home to do so? Tap into peer accountability. Often, they can motivate each other more effectively than you can. Also, make sure you celebrate progress; students will naturally want to be part of the celebration.

What about "Accountability Partners"?

Many people benefit from having a person they can account to for progress on their measures. One or two partners might be logistically easier to handle than a team WIG Session. An "Accountability Partner" can help define WIGs and lead measures, track scoreboards, and meet together to assess progress. How to put those partnerships together? It can vary by classroom and age of student and classroom composition. You are the expert in your classroom. If your students would benefit from building a rapport and trust with the same partner, consider assigning Accountability Partners. If you'd rather do quick check-ins, consider "turn and talk" or "elbow" partners.

How often should Accountability Partners meet?

Minimally, once a week, consistent with the principle of the cadence of accountability.

Can students have an Accountability Partners that is not the same age or grade?

Why not? Ensure students are able to meet once a week and the conversation will be mutually beneficial.

How long do Accountability Partners meet?

Five to fifteen minutes is usually enough time for a meaningful conversation. When the students understand the cadence of accountability and it has been modeled for them, the partnership will be smoother and more fruitful.

When do we celebrate with students?

Make celebrations part of your regular routines. If you review your classroom scoreboard weekly, and there is progress, celebrate it! When students meet with their Accountability Partner and they complete their lead measures or score a personal best, celebrate that too. The goal is to keep everyone engaged and motivated.

What are some ways to celebrate student achievements?

High fives, special cheers, recognition during school announcements, certificates, stickers, an "I met my goal" lanyard, an extra recess—try these and many more ideas for celebrations. Ask the students how they would like to celebrate. They'll tell you!

What is your best advice for ensuring 4DX is successful in my classroom or school?

Model, model, model. Keep having conversations about the 4 Disciplines process with your students and faculty. Don't expect everything to go smoothly from the start; processes take time to perfect and a lot of trial and error. Don't give up! Achieving your Wildly Important Goals will feel amazing.

So Now What?

Reflection: Sean Covey
From Unpredictable to Predictable

While we were writing this book, I went into a local car dealership to lease a car. The gentlemen who approached me asked my name and upon hearing the last name of Covey asked if I worked at Franklin-Covey. I said that I did. He then asked, "Have you ever heard of The 4 Disciplines of Execution?"

I laughed and told him that I was one of the coauthors of the original book. His face lit up.

"Hey, it's so good to meet you. You gotta know that I'm a total believer in the 4 Disciplines. I am the general manager of this dealership and I was given responsibility over it because I did so well with my other dealership. And I turned my other dealership around using the 4 Disciplines. This stuff really works!"

"That's awesome!" I replied. "I'm so happy to hear that it's working for you. How's it going with this dealership?"

"This is a struggling dealership," he continued, "and I've only been in charge for a few months now, but things are turning around quickly thanks to this approach. It's changing everything! Take a look at the scoreboard of my sales team. They are crushing it."

He pointed to the scoreboard on a nearby wall. It had leads and lags and you could tell who was winning or losing at a glance, just like we teach. It was compelling. And then he said the most profound thing of all.

"For the first time, my sales team knows exactly what to do to sell more cars. They can now predict and control how many cars they sell each month. It used to be an art. Now it's predictable. They have figured out the lead measures for selling cars. They know that they have to make two hundred touchpoints through social media, email, calls, and other outlets to sell one car. I have former salespeople who quit and who are coming back to work for me because they finally know that they can win!"

I was so touched to see the impact these principles had had upon his business and to see the excitement in his eyes and the eyes of his team. It was tangible. This man knew exactly what he needed to do to turn around his second car dealership and he was doing it, using a methodology based on the principles of getting things done: focus, leverage, engagement, and accountability. He had the tools he needed to win and they were all within his control.

And to top it off, to show his enthusiasm, he even gave me a big discount off my lease. I kind of felt guilty about accepting his offer but I got over it quickly and took it anyway, smiling all the way home.

A Final Word

These 4 Disciplines truly work. How could they not? Once you understand these laws of execution would you ever turn away from them? Why would you ever set ten vague goals when you know that one or two well-crafted goals work better? Why would you ever focus on lag measures when you know that nothing changes until you apply the leverage of lead measures? Why would you ever run your school or your district or your university without a public scoreboard which engages people and lets them track if you're winning or losing? Why would you ever neglect having a cadence of accountability when you know that things fall apart without it? Truly, 4DX is a better way to operate. Ultimately, everyone wants to win, improve, and get better. And your chances of winning go way up if you have a framework for getting things done.

When we walk into a school and see a big public scoreboard posted in the main hall that reads something like—*Our WIG is to improve our attendance from 89 percent to 95 percent by May 30*—and then see aligned scoreboards in each classroom, we simply know that the school is going to achieve the WIG. When you have a common goal shared by everyone in the school, how could it not?

It is so difficult to improve a school. There are so many priorities to juggle and stakeholders to please. And there is always so much noise from the whirlwind. How in the world can we improve behavior, attendance, reading scores, graduation rates, and the culture of the school? It can almost seem impossible, as if it would take a miracle to effect change. This cartoon illustrates how so many educators feel.

But it doesn't have to be this way. The principles of execution can make it otherwise. They offer a predictable and influenceable methodology for accomplishing any goal by any team. We spoke earlier about Collective Teacher Efficacy, which is the hope and belief that by working together we can create change. Our experience is that the 4 Disciplines of Execution create collective teacher efficacy. Just like it did for the car dealership general manager, the 4DX methodology offers you and your team a hope and a belief that change can and will happen.

So now what? Now that you understand the 4 Disciplines, what will you do about them? We hope that you do a lot. Our quest to solve the problem of execution began twenty years before this book was written. A survey we got our hands on at that time told us that the top challenge of leaders was execution, or getting things done as a team. It's easy to set a lofty goal, but hard to get it done, especially when it involves a lot of people.

So, we spent a decade trying to solve this problem, and after a lot of trial and error and deep thinking, we painstakingly stumbled upon these principles and disciplines. We purposely use the word "stumble" because there was a little bit of serendipity and luck involved, for sure. And to be frank, we've been a little surprised and humbled to discover how transformational these disciplines are. As a result, 4DX is now being used by thousands of entities, including large Fortune 500 companies, small business owners, government agencies, colleges and universities, and public and private schools around the globe. We hope now that they will be used by you.

We want to wish you success in your work as educators. Outside of the work we do within our own families, the work you do with our students is the most noble and important work happening in the world. You are shaping people's lives forever. The amount of influence you can have on the one is incalculable. Each of us as authors can point to teachers who significantly altered our lives for good.

Because we want you to succeed, we strongly encourage you to practice these Disciplines, whether you're a teacher, a principal, a superintendent, or a chancellor. They work. So please, narrow your focus. Identify and act on the lead measures that will move the needle. Keep score and let everyone know if you're winning or losing. And create a culture of accountability. Then sit back, relax, and watch your scoreboard light up.

Gallery of Scoreboards

To help give you ideas for your own scoreboards, here is a gallery of real scoreboards educators have used to motivate progress toward WIGs.

School Scoreboard (Public)

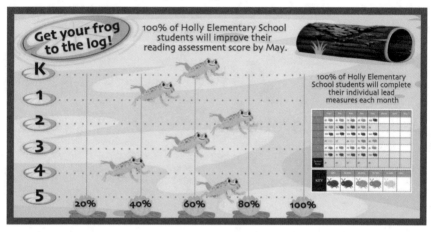

Classroom Scoreboard (Public)

Student Scoreboard (Private)

Name _Jasmine Dalton_

My Reading WIG

I will go from Level _N_ to Level _P_
on my reading assessment by the end
of the second marking period.

Act on the Lead Measures		Key
1	I will read independently every night for 20 minutes.	●
2	I will read out loud with my reading buddy for 15 minutes 3 times per week.	○

Monday	Tuesday	Wednesday	Thursday	Friday	Reflection
1 ● ●	2 ●	3 ● ○	4 ● ●	5 ●	😊
8 ● ○	9 ○	10 ● ●	11 ●	12	😐
15	16 ●	17 ○	18	19 ○	🙁
22	23	24	25	26	

Create a Cadence of Accountability	
My Accountability Partner:	Sarah
My Celebration:	Extra Recess

Student Scoreboard (Private)

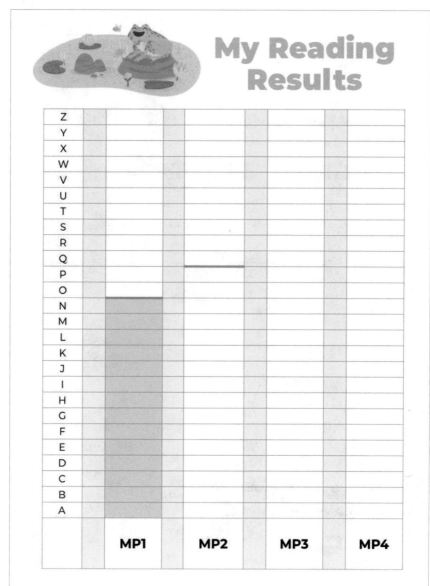

Teacher Scoreboard (Private)

Mr. Guerriero's Professional WIG
I will go from 43% of my students reading on or above grade level to 83% by May 2021.

February Lead Measure Scoreboard				
Monday	Tuesday	Wednesday	Thursday	Friday
1 ● ●●	2 ●● ●	3 ● ●●	4 ● ●●	5 ● ○
8 ○○	9 ● ○	10 ●● ○	11 ●●●●	12 ●●
15 ●●●○	16 ●●○	17 ●●●○	18 ●●○	19 ●●○
22 ●●○	23 ●●○	24 ●●	25 ●●○	26 ●●

Bar chart: MP1 = 43%, MP2 = 53%, MP3, MP4

Mr. Guerriero's Professional WIG Lead Measures and Proficiency Scoreboard

Exceeds Standard			Lead Measures:	Key
Anita Christian	Mark Helen	Lina		●
Meets Standard			**Lead Measures:**	
Jose Laura Azami Kamal	Benjamin Malik Olivia Aisha	Arthur Mia Laila		●
Approaching Standard			**Lead Measures:**	
Sarah Dylan Evander	Jasmine Ethan Justin	Emma Idris Nasir		●
Far From Standard			**Lead Measures:**	
Harper Matthew	Alex Nia	Evelyn		○

The teacher will record a specific, differentiated lead measure for each group in the lead measure column.

School Scoreboard (Public)

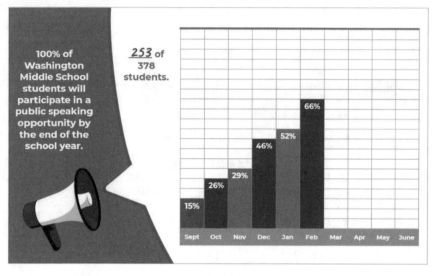

Grade Level Scoreboard (Public)

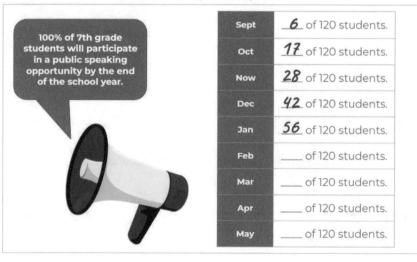

Classroom Scoreboard (Public)

> **100% of Ms. Smith's 7-3 Homeroom will participate in a public speaking opportunity this year.**

KEY — Participated in 1 opportunity · Participated in 2-5 opportunities · Participated in 6+ opportunities

Casey	Gao	Rohit	Malia	Karson	Samitha	Camille	Ibrahim
Marie	Nyla	Lyric	Jake	Jeff	Izabella	Alex	Jaiden
Lilliana	Angelo	D'Shawn	Luka	Hector	Zara	Havin	Jane

Month	Percent
Sept	12%
Oct	21%
Now	29%
Dec	50%
Jan	55%
Feb	64%
Mar	
Apr	
May	

Student's Individual WIG (Private)

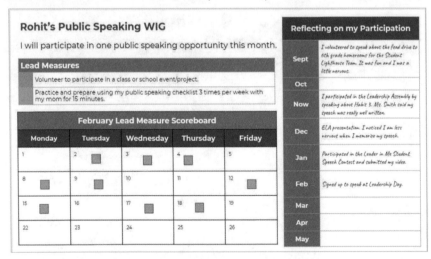

Rohit's Public Speaking WIG

I will participate in one public speaking opportunity this month.

Lead Measures

Volunteer to participate in a class or school event/project.

Practice and prepare using my public speaking checklist 3 times per week with my mom for 15 minutes.

February Lead Measure Scoreboard

Monday	Tuesday	Wednesday	Thursday	Friday
1	2 ■	3 ■	4 ■	5
8 ■	9 ■	10	11	12 ■
15 ■	16	17 ■	18 ■	19
22	23	24	25	26

Reflecting on my Participation

Month	Reflection
Sept	I volunteered to speak about the food drive to 6th grade homerooms for the Student Lighthouse Team. It was fun and I was a little nervous.
Oct	
Now	I participated in the Leadership Assembly by speaking about Habit 3. Ms. Smith said my speech was really well written.
Dec	ELA presentation. I noticed I am less nervous when I memorize my speech.
Jan	Participated in the Leader in Me Student Speech Contest and submitted my video.
Feb	Signed up to speak at Leadership Day.
Mar	
Apr	
May	

School Scoreboard (Public)

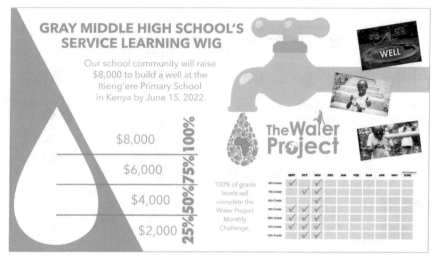

Advisory Period Scoreboard (Public)

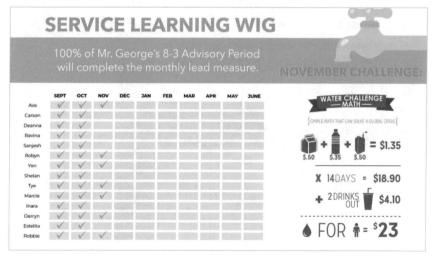

Student Scoreboard (Private)

My Service Learning WIG
I will complete *The Water Project* lead measures every month.

Advisory Period Accountability Partner:	Deanna

Month	Lead Measure Activity	Completed By:	Reflection
Sept	Read *The Long Walk to Water*		
Oct	Problem Based Learning Project on the water crisis in Africa		
Nov	Repost social media content to raise awareness		
Dec	Participate in the Water Math Challenge		
Jan	Participate in the Water Math Challenge		
Feb	Get ___ sponsors for the Walk for Water Fundraising Event		
Mar	Get ___ sponsors for the Walk for Water Fundraising Event		
Apr	Get ___ sponsors for the Walk for Water Fundraising Event		
May	Attend the Walk for Water Fundraising Event		
June	Sign up for a Leadership Day Leadership Role		

Endnotes

1   Theodore R. Sizer, *Horace's Compromise: The Dilemma of the American High School*, New York: Houghton-Mifflin, 2004, 20-21

2   Doris Santoro, "The Problem With Stories About Teacher 'Burnout,'" *Phi Delta Kappan*, Nov. 25, 2019.

3   Mike Schmoker, *Focus: Elevating the Essentials to Dramatically Improve Student Learning*, Alexandria, VA: ASCD, 2018, 4.

4   Elaine Weiss, Don Long, "Market-Oriented Reforms' Rhetoric Trumps Reality," Schott Foundation, Apr. 22, 2013, 7.

5   Stevenson, Isobel (2019). An improvement plan is not enough — you need a strategy. *Phi Delta Kappan, 100* (6), 60-64.

6   Galvin, Mike and Parsley, Danette, "Turning Failure Into Opportunity," *Educational Leadership*, vol. 62, no. 9 (Summer 2005). http://www.ascd.org/publications/educational-leadership/summer05/vol62/num09/Turning-Failure-Into-Opportunity.aspx

7   John Naish, "Is Multitasking Bad for Your Brain?" *DailyMail.com*, August 11, 2009.

8   Nicholas Carr, "Does the Internet Make You Dumber?" *Wall Street Journal Online*, June 5, 2010.

9   Goodwin, Bryan, *Simply Better: Doing What Matters Most to Change the Odds*, Alexandria, VA: ASCD, 2011, 124-129; *Noteworthy Perspectives: Success in Sight*, Denver: MCREL, 2006, 4.

10   "John F. Kennedy and NASA," NASA.gov, May 22, 2015. https://www.nasa.gov/feature/john-f-kennedy-and-nasa

11   Damian Cooper, "Avoiding the DRIP Problem," *Fresh Grade*, blog, n.d. https://freshgrade.com/blog/avoiding-the-drip-phenomenon-by-damian-cooper/

12   Andrew Stott and Carmen Neustaedter, "Analysis of Gamification in Education," http://clab.iat.sfu.ca/pubs/Stott-Gamification.pdf

13   Duke, Daniel and Michael Salmonowicz, "Key Decisions of a First-year 'Turnaround' Principal," *Educational Management Administration Leadership*, vol. 38, no. 1 (Jan. 5, 2010), 37-51.

14   Lynch, Matthew. "Five Major Barriers to Sustainable School improvement," *The EAdvocate*, Feb. 28, 2016. https://www.theedadvocate.org/5-major-barriers-to-sustainable-school-improvement/

15   See T. J. Hoogsteen, "Collective efficacy: toward a new narrative of its development and role in achievement," *Palgrave Communications*, vol. 6, no. 2 (2020).

Acknowledgements

Achieving measurable results in schools through the 4 Disciplines of Execution would not be possible without the over 20 years of development, practice, and refinement from so many associates at FranklinCovey. In particular, we wanted to thank the following:

Thank you to the late Jim Stuart who deserves more credit than anyone for the foundational ideas behind the 4 Disciplines. Thank you for showing us the way, Jim, and for coining the phrase "wildly important."

Thank you to our colleagues Chris McChesney, Mark Josie, and Jim Huling, the original practitioners, who refined and polished this content over many years. Your brilliance has impacted thousands of organizations across the world, including schools.

Thank you to our talented friend and colleague Breck England, who not only shaped the original 4 Disciplines content, but also served as the chief writing officer on this book, helping to blend our voices into a coherent whole while adding valuable insights of his own.

Thank you to our ever-patient project manager, Holly Stewart, who kept our team organized and moving forward, and always did it with a smile.

Thank you to Jody Karr, Mel Wise, James Coleman, and Catherine DiGioia-Weinfeld for your artistic excellence. Your creative fingerprints appear throughout this book, bringing life and color to the content.

Thank you to our world class FranklinCovey coaching team, led by the visionary Shelly Rider, for your invaluable contributions in shaping

4DX for education. Your superb implementation coaching and dedication to helping schools achieve results is unparalleled.

Thank you to our international team, led by Bill McIntyre and Brooke Judd, for your feedback and insights after implementing 4DX in hundreds of schools throughout the world.

Thank you to our superb product development and marketing teams, led by Aaron Ashby and Zac Cheney, who have done so much to advance and promote the 4 Disciplines content over many years.

Finally, thank you to the students, teachers, principals, superintendents, and higher education leaders who believe in the power of 4DX and work tirelessly to implement the Disciplines to achieve their Wildly Important Goals. Thank you for trusting us, believing in the process, and sharing your greatness. Most of all, thank you for believing in your students and supporting them to reach greater heights.

Index

About the Authors

SEAN COVEY is a business executive, author, speaker, and innovator. He is president of FranklinCovey Education and is devoted to transforming education through FranklinCovey's whole school improvement process called *Leader in Me*, which is now in over 5,000 K–12 schools and 50 countries throughout the world. As the former head of Innovations for FranklinCovey, Sean was the original architect of *The 4 Disciplines of Execution* methodology and has been an avid practitioner and promoter of the methodology ever since.

Sean is a *New York Times* bestselling author and has authored or coauthored several books, including the *Wall Street Journal* #1 Business Bestseller, *The 4 Disciplines of Execution*, *The 6 Most Important Decisions You'll Ever Make*, *The 7 Habits of Happy Kids*, *The Leader in Me*, and *The 7 Habits of Highly Effective Teens*, which has been translated into 30 languages and sold over eight million copies worldwide. He is a versatile keynoter who regularly speaks at education and business events, and has appeared on numerous radio and TV shows and print media.

Sean graduated with honors from BYU with a bachelor's degree in English, and later earned his MBA from Harvard Business School. As the starting quarterback for BYU, he led his team to two bowl games and was twice selected as the ESPN's Most Valuable Player of the Game. Sean and his family founded and run a global, non-profit charity called Bridle Up Hope, whose mission is to inspire hope, confidence, and resilience in struggling young women through equestrian training.

Born in Belfast, Ireland, Sean's favorite activities include going to movies, working out, hanging out with his kids, riding his motorcycle, coaching youth football, producing short films, and writing books. Sean and his wife, Rebecca, live with their children in the shadows of the Rocky Mountains.

LYNN FAIRBROTHER KOSINSKI

As an education coach and consultant heavily involved in product development, Lynn Fairbrother Kosinski is a 4DX thought leader for Franklin-Covey's Education Division. She is the lead architect for many of the 4DX solutions and has facilitated 4DX content to clients worldwide.

Lynn has over three decades of teaching, leadership, and consulting experience. Prior to joining FranklinCovey, Lynn spent over 25 years in K–12 education, starting in the elementary classroom. Lynn was named an elementary principal at age 25, launching a long administrative career. Thereafter she gained valuable additional experience as a middle school principal, eventually moving to central office roles as Director of Elementary Education, Director of Secondary Education and ultimately, Assistant Superintendent of Curriculum of Instruction.

Lynn holds a bachelor's degree from the University of Michigan and a master's degree from Oakland University in Curriculum, Instruction, and Leadership. She is a doctoral student at Central Michigan University concentrating in educational technology.

MEG THOMPSON is the Vice President and General Manager of FranklinCovey Education and partners directly with K–12 districts and schools to identify and develop the potential of their staff and students.

Meg has served as a consultant and executive coach on strategy execution on FranklinCovey's Organizational Sales Team, where she was instrumental in the early development of FranklinCovey's leadership solution, The 4 Disciplines of Execution (4DX). She has improved organizational productivity and performance with Fortune 100 clients in the pharmaceutical, technology, and oil industries.

Meg has a BA in Industrial Psychology and Computer Science from La-Salle University, an MA in Human Organization Science from Villanova University, and is certified in Executive Coaching through Columbia University.

About FranklinCovey Education

For nearly three decades, FranklinCovey Education, a division of FranklinCovey, has been one of the world's most prominent and trusted providers of educational-leadership programs and transformational processes. FranklinCovey's programs, books, and content have been utilized by thousands of public and private primary, secondary, and post-secondary schools and institutions, including educational service centers and vocational colleges in over 50 countries.

The *Leader in Me* is Franklin Covey's whole school transformation process and is being implemented in over 5,000 K–12 schools around the world. It teaches 21st century leadership and life skills to students and creates a culture of student empowerment based on the idea that every child can be a leader.

The *Leader in Me* is aligned with best-in-class content and concepts practiced by global education thought leaders. It provides a logical, sequential, and balanced process to help schools proactively design the culture that reflects their vision of the ideal school.

The FranklinCovey Education team is primarily composed of outstanding former teachers and administrators from various educational levels and entities.

About FranklinCovey

FranklinCovey is a global, public company specializing in building leaders at every level, from the classroom to the boardroom and everything in between. We are the world leader in helping organizations achieve results that require lasting changes in human behavior, often the most difficult challenge any organization faces. When accomplished, it is also the most durable competitive advantage.

We provide content, tools, methodology, training and thought leadership, all based on a foundation of unshakeable principles and proven practices.

Our ultimate aim is to deliver not just incremental but transformational results. Our expanding reach now extends to more than 150 countries, with over 2,000 associates working toward our common mission of enabling greatness in people and organizations everywhere.

For more information about *Leader in Me* or other FranklinCovey Education offerings, contact us at:

educate@franklincovey.com

800-236-5291

LeaderinMe.org

FranklinCovey | EDUCATION

Utilize 4DX in your schools to achieve your most important goals.

Thousands of *Leader in Me* schools and districts around the globe use 4DX to help their teams execute on their highest priorities in the midst of the whirlwind. We find when we teach 4DX to administrators and then empower them to teach and implement the process with their educators, the results can be game-changing.

Unleash the potential of your staff and students with *Leader in Me* **and** *The 4 Disciplines of Execution.*

www.LeaderinMe.org
1-800-236-5291

LeaderinMe.

Developing Life-Ready Leaders®

LeaderinMe®

Grow College, Career, and Life-Readiness Skills

Leader in Me high school leadership courses guide young adults in developing the skills they need to adapt and thrive in the future, putting them on the path to accomplishing their career and post-secondary goals.

Visit LeaderinMe.org to learn how to bring *Leader in Me* to your school.

Other Books By Sean Covey

- *The 4 Disciplines of Execution*
- *The 7 Habits of Highly Effective People: 30th Anniversary Edition*
- *The 7 Habits of Highly Effective Teens*
- *The 7 Habits of Happy Kids*
- *The 7 Habits of Happy Kids: Boxed Set*
- *The 6 Most Important Decisions You'll Ever Make*

Available wherever books are sold.

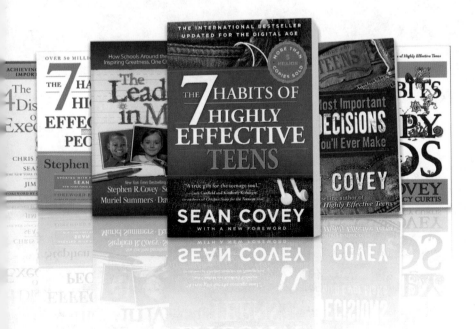